MAN—IFOLD WISDOM

Also by Wesley Carr and published by SPCK:

Brief Encounters: Pastoral Ministry through the Occasional Offices New Library of Pastoral Care (1985)

The Pastor as Theologian: The Integration of Pastoral Ministry, Theology and Discipleship New Library of Pastoral Care (1989)

Ministry and the Media (1990)

Wesley Carr

MANIFOLD WISDOM

The Churches' Ministry in
the New Age

First published in Great Britain 1991
SPCK
Holy Trinity Church
Marylebone Road
London NW1 4DU

British Library Cataloguing-in-Publication Data.

A catalogue record for this book
is available from the British Library.

ISBN 0 281 04550 X

Typeset by Pioneer Associates, Perthshire
Printed in Great Britain by
Mackays of Chatham plc.

For Clive and Val Simmonds

with thanks for much friendship
and for forbearance during the writing in
Spain, Summer 1990

To me, though I am the very least of all the saints, this grace was given, to preach to the Gentiles the unsearchable riches of Christ, and to make all men see what is the plan of the mystery hidden for ages in God who created all things; that through the church the manifold wisdom of God might now be made known to the principalities and powers in the heavenly places.

PAUL'S LETTER TO THE EPHESIANS 3.8–10

Contents

Preface

If you go into any bookshop today and look for books on Christianity, you will usually find them under the general heading of 'Religion'. That is not so surprising. What may cause a shock, however, is the material with which books on the Bible, the Christian faith and the Church now keep company. There will be volumes on the occult, Tarot cards, crystals, and the channelling of spirits. Some will be old texts from the wisdom of antiquity, including alchemy. Magic will certainly be represented, along with witchcraft. Others will sound very modern, written in 'psychobabble', that mélange of languages derived from counselling, therapy, psychology and sociology. There will almost certainly be treatises on spirituality. The contribution of women will be noticeable.

The bookseller has not made a mistake: all of these topics and more are today's 'religion'. Christianity's place among them is a parable for today's Church, which finds itself, perhaps as never since the second century, influenced by and influencing a welter of beliefs, some more fantastic than others, but all taken seriously by their devotees.

One phrase in particular has emerged, under the umbrella of which many of these ideas cohere – 'The New Age'. There are any number of books and magazines in which it appears. Bantam Books, for example, publish a New Age Library. Journals abound, although most of them are ephemeral. The annual festival of Mind–Body–Spirit offers the ideas to any who come. But the 'New Age' is indefinable. The best that can be offered might be:

A leaderless but powerful network is working to bring about radical change in the United States. Its members have broken with certain key elements of Western thought, and they may even have broken continuity with history. This network is the Aquarian Conspiracy. It is a conspiracy without a political doctrine, without a manifesto.[1]

If the phenomenon originated anywhere in particular it was in the USA. But it is increasingly influential in Europe and is to be found in Great Britain. Television Channel Four thought it significant enough to devote a series to it early in 1991. The New Age contributes to the context in which Christian ministers now have to work.

It would be a challenge to write a summary and interpretation of something so nebulous. But that is not my aim. The story of the bookshop is the story of today's Christian ministry. The churches may wish to take note of the New Age phenomenon and adopt stances towards it. Predictably already some see in it an anti-Christian movement to be resisted.[2] Others, like St James', Piccadilly, will give it a home without necessarily endorsing all its aspects. The New Age itself includes various assessments of Christianity. Some participants see this old religion as something which could be redeemed and on which to build; others regard it as at best the defunct religion and at worst a malign hindrance to enlightenment.

The debate is not very exciting and scarcely worth joining, since many of the same views are frequently expressed, often more coherently, within the Church itself. More significant in the final decade of this century and millennium is what the existence of the New Age may represent to the Church about the context of belief and expectation in which its gospel has to be interpreted. Unless ministers can have some grasp of this, their teaching and leading will seem even more irrelevant to most people.

Instead, therefore, of attempting an evaluation of the New Age phenomenon, I have tried to discern some distinctive messages its existence might send to the Church. These turn out to be particularly important in three areas of life – spirituality, healing or therapy, and our relationship to nature. There is, however, another more important indicator for ministers. It emerges from thinking about the New Age that, while the Christian tradition still has rich resources with which to speak to the condition of people in the late twentieth century, these chiefly reside in its theology rather than the activities of the churches.

Theology and action are, of course, inextricably linked. But it seems that the most important development that the churches could make in this decade would be to recover confidence in the discipline of theological thinking, affirming the importance of the minister first as a theological thinker and only secondly as a pastor and teacher. When the old nostrums work neither for the church nor for the world, the time has not necessarily come to leap towards new ones. The first test has to be whether the rich resources of the Christian tradition are being explored and exploited to the full. I hope to have suggested some ways, pointed up by the spiritual search exemplified in the New Age, in which they are not and in which ministers, particularly in their role as local theologians, can work constructively.

The book does not contain a list of answers to the dilemmas of contemporary ministry. Even less does it suggest how to respond to the questions being proposed by the New Age. But the struggle to which I invite the reader is that, I suggest, in which the Church can profitably for the gospel be engaged for at least the next ten years.

Wesley Carr
Bristol
January 1991

NOTES

1 'New Age Movement', in Eileen Barker. *A Dictionary of New Religious Movements* (London. HMSO, 1989), p. 188.
2 Michael Cole. Jim Graham. Tony Higton and David Lewis. *What is the New Age?* (London. Hodder & Stoughton. 1990).

1 | Towards 2000

When a millennium ends, normal anxieties are reinforced. We, of all generations, are accustomed to live with crises. But they feel intensified by the sensed end of so long a period as a thousand years. The significance of the end of a century feels enhanced. The shift from 'nineteen hundred' to 'two thousand' is more enigmatic than a mere change of centuries. So as the last decade of the twentieth century progresses we shall be bombarded with reviews of the turning points of other centuries, and especially of each millennium. Such epochs become moments of felt cataclysm – serious ending coupled with hopeful new possibilities. All, whatever their particular beliefs, share a sense of a new age.

This time, however, the phrase 'new age' has already been claimed. Some people describe themselves as 'New Agers'. Publications to do with this new era proliferate. The decline in the public importance assigned to the Christian faith and its symbols in the West means not so much that there is a spiritual vacuum as that we no longer possess a common language for articulating spiritual longing. Christians have hitherto reckoned that their faith provided this. We could describe human experience in terms of salvation, redemption, and new life. We have been more wary of the ways in which it might also provide an eschatological vocabulary for human longings and aspirations. Even in this century Western literature and art have drawn largely on Judaeo-Christian imagery as a vehicle for their expression. We are now, however, entering a period when this can no longer be assumed. A new religious language may (one cannot be sure) be emerging. Certainly there is a feeling that it may be necessary.

The context of the New Age

Whatever the case – and it is difficult to be precise when we are standing so close to events and change – as we face a new millennium (which is still counted as the 'Christian Era'), the Church needs to consider the issues which the New Age represents. Unlike some historical challenges to the Church this one is not obviously in competition for power and dominance over people's lives. Nor is it the presentation of an alternative theological system. These are more characteristic of the New Religious Movements, which are self-consciously organized bodies to which people firmly adhere or by which they are held.[1] The New Age is not a movement: it is a phenomenon. Any struggle with Christianity or other mainstream religions, therefore, is about the nature of a synthesis of thought and consequent action which will enable both individuals and the world to survive. It is a confrontation over the ultimate issues of God, creation (nature and humankind) and salvation. While some offerings of the New Age may appear bizarre, and to Christians not especially new, the issues raised are serious and will be central to the life of the Christian Church during the coming decade. Unless, therefore, ministers are aware of them, their ministry will feel, both to them and to the people among whom they move, increasingly remote.

The term 'New Age' is an accurate description. The word 'age' is exactly that which is familiar to students of the New Testament and early Christian history – *aion*: '*Aion* is a term of fluid sense, popular perhaps because of the vague suggestion of the unknowable.'[2] It refers less to a length of time than to its quality, and links the present with the future, usually in an apocalyptic setting. Today's proponents of New Age thinking are developing a similar stance.

The end of a millennium is a fixed moment. New Age ideas are more fluid. But together they create, however momentarily, a new context for the Church. Reflection is appropriate in the circumstances, although it is noticeable that the churches' first formal response to the end of this century seems to have been more aggressive than reflective. It has been claimed as 'The Decade of Evangelism' (or Evangelization). Whether this is an attempt to recall the lapsed or convert the inattentive, evangelism is less about new thinking than renewed application of old ideas. Hence the Decade of Evangelism may be regarded as another facet of the conservatism which imbues the churches. The end of a millennium generally arouses primitive anxieties which encourage conservatism; but it should not do so in those who seek to share God's eternal perspective. But whatever the Church's stance, ministers will need to take serious account of the context within which they are set and to which they contribute, whether the Decade of Evangelism represents a creative advance or a defensive reaction.

For the past two millennia in the West Christianity has created the religious context. Today, however, it finds itself participating in, not setting the agenda for, a wider religious programme. In part this is because religions from the rest of the world have penetrated the consciousness of people in the West. Occasional instances of this happening in history can be produced, such as when Islam invaded southern Spain. But the general awareness, which today pervades people's consciousness, that there are religions other than Christianity represents a new situation. Travel, the media and other means of communication, which make the world feel a more intimate place than hitherto, play their part. But this awareness of other religions in addition leads to an increased sensitivity about the whole idea of 'religion'.

Coupled with this sense of religiosity, amid which Christian claims to uniqueness sit uneasily, is another major question. Are the secular assumptions which have dominated thought during this century losing their hold? If so, is the process of secularization itself in decline? To offer a confident answer might be seen as thinly disguised triumphalism – we Christians knew it would eventually turn out all right for God and for Christianity in particular. Such an attitude implies a return to what are believed to have been old values and traditional Christian practices. But that belief is a delusion. Whatever happens to the Christian Church, one of its lasting memorials will be the explosion of knowledge and understanding – including its dark side – which has followed Christian faith in God. Such belief, therefore, can never be in a settled state: the generation of change is implicit in the Christian faith.

The culturally pluralist forms of society, which allow, and may even encourage, religious and secular diversity, also owe their existence to a degree to the influence of the Christian gospel.[3] This is evident in Europe, but even more so in the USA. There no single religion can lay formal claim to be dominant, even if the motto 'In God we Trust' is used on their coinage and a so-called 'National Cathedral' has been built in Washington. Yet these instances may themselves be seen as specific symbols of a stance which, even if forgotten, was enshrined in the founding deed of the nation. This was based upon Christian principles, albeit established in opposition to the way that these had evolved in Europe.

We have recently discovered that the relationship between secularization and religion is more complex than was at one time thought. Predictions of rapid change, such as were sometimes made in the 1960s and 1970s, have proved misguided. One thing, however, has become clear: whatever changes occur, these will not involve a return to some notionally 'old' gospel or simple Christianity. From time to time this is urged as the solution to the decline of the Church's apparent impact. In some contexts this belief claims the plausibility of success: churches appear to be full because they offer such assurance and naively claim (and some with equal naivety acknowledge) that this is the sole reason for their achievement. Television religion in the USA is another instance, where the trappings of success and the ideology of entertainment become confused but for some imply that old-time religious simplicity is self-authenticating. But neither of these phenomena looks like a major reversal of the complex trends of the late twentieth century.[4] Working ministers are unlikely to be seduced by them for long.

The academic debate about the evidence for what is

happening and whether a major cultural shift is occurring is important. Such global interpretation is necessary. But for the Church's ministers the issue is more immediate and they have to adopt stances towards it. On the one hand, they proclaim a faith which they believe profoundly interprets the core questions of human existence: How can people live together? What is the nature of God? How should people behave? Can we survive potential ecological disaster? On the other hand, they represent a religion which, it is widely believed, cannot be relevant to these issues, because its adherents are largely blamed for the malaise from which people are seeking escape. This ambiguity alone gives peculiar poignancy to the prospect of the churches' assigning priority to evangelism during the decade which ends the millennium.

The state of the Church

What then is the state of the Church as it enters this decade and faces the new age? One mark is a tendency towards a renewed emphasis on the local congregation. This seems to lead to a sectarian attitude at all levels of church life. The term 'sectarian' is not here used in a technical sense. The sociological debate continues.[5] But underneath it many ministers feel that the churches in general are, for whatever reason, becoming preoccupied with issues of self-identity. The experienced vicar, for example, finds himself less able to function in the public arena of the parish because of the demands of the congregation (and consequential organizational requirements of the church at other levels of its functioning) that he devote his time to them. This development is, whatever the rationalizations offered for it, essentially defensive and not in the long term a sign of confidence. Parallel to this, however, there may also be discerned a more diffuse but confident assent that there is a future for the churches, provided that they display capacity for change. In 1987 David Edwards surveyed the scene and concluded:

Towards the end of his [Paul Johnson's] *A History of the Modern World* (1983) he wrote: 'What is important in history is not only the events that occur but the events that obstinately do not occur. The outstanding non-event of modern times was the failure of religious belief to disappear' . . . I conclude that belief in God through Jesus, which certainly has failed to disappear, is likely to inspire future Christians both to respect the diversity which God blesses and to seek the communion which is commanded by love.[6]

One expression of this confidence has been the recovery of the value of the local church, which should not be equated with the congregation. This reclaiming seems to be chiefly concerned with a need to discover where explorable authority resides and where humanity can be discovered. On the large scale, for instance, although there have recently been signs of increasing centralization in the Roman Catholic Church, we may also discern an affirmation of the national and local significance of churches. This shift marked Vatican II, the effects of which have not been wholly obscured, and, in the Anglican Communion, the most recent Lambeth Conference. Within congregations there has been a matching emphasis upon the effectiveness of the small group. This is sometimes an expression of the search for intimacy, but it can also at another level be a reaffirmation of something significant in human life generally.

For example, during the 1960s and 1970s the Church of England was for a period almost eager to dismantle its parochial system, by which it relates its life to local communities.[7] It was argued that teams of clergy and complex collections of committed individuals in different groupings would create the lively new church.[8] Leaving the dormitory parish, clergy would find new ministries in industry, commerce, education and elsewhere. This has not happened. Indeed a style of life is beginning to re-emerge in the nation which gives renewed (though different) prominence to home and leisure, the locus of the parish. Some even suggest that this change will require us to adjust our basic assumptions about work and the way people order their lives rather than, as some thought, *vice versa*.[9]

The rediscovery of locality (in all its senses) in the life of the churches is matched by a new shape to their wider context. The organized denominations struggle to find an order which puts what is local in its proper place, without assigning it total significance. In the language of the Church of England, the question is how to be parochially ordered (i.e. structured for potential engagement with all people) without becoming parochial (i.e. small-minded). One consequence has been the creation of different tiers of church life – deaneries, synods, districts and so on. In practice, however, these seem to be ignored by the most enthusiastic people, who generate their own level of supra-parochial life.

Core members of their local church find spiritual renewal in different forms of association, which may come into being once or twice a year. Pilgrimages to Walsingham or Glastonbury, meetings such as Spring Harvest and Greenbelt, the continuance of old meetings like the Keswick Convention, and attendance at such places as Iona or Lee Abbey, are all renewed marks of contemporary Christian life, along with the plethora of locally based courses and study groups. Clergy, including the most senior, seek spiritual, emotional and professional support in their membership of cells, to which they give priority. Retreats and study days have become more popular, as people seek something beyond the local church which, however, does not destroy for them its significance.

These activities are a mark of something more widespread: people seem to seek to believe something without wishing to take on the real or imagined commitment of belonging.[10] On closer examination, however, they may be compartmentalizing the different dimensions of their spiritual experience without expecting to find it fully catered for in any one component. In other words, they immerse themselves for fixed periods in religious activity which is both complete (fully satisfactory for the moment) and inadequate (since there are other dimensions to their lives which have to be acknowledged). For many the balance is not yet right, but the signs are there that this may become a norm of what is meant by 'church membership'.

One result is that minimal attention is (and will be) paid to church 'rules', whether canon law or merely customs. Hitherto anarchic behaviour has been issue centred – the ordination of women, for instance, or reception of communion in other churches than one's own. Such 'disobedience' as there has been has been on the whole contained within the context of an individual's private belief. The main opportunity for pushing the official boundaries has come through ecumenical activity. Local Ecumenical Projects provide 'legitimate' occasions for such rule breaking. These formal entities, however, are probably the last flowering of an outdated ecumenism and will give place to looser associations during this decade. Such a shift should provide church leaders, who will inevitably be first the local pastor or vicar, with intriguing problems of what, if anything, it means to belong to a specific church and accept any discipline.

The issue is not new. But to date reflection and action on it has been the prerogative of the few. In the nineteen sixties, for example, Charles Davis wrote:

> If someone now asks me whether I am a Catholic, I do not know how to answer. I know that I do not fulfil the requirements for membership laid down in Canon Law, nor do I give assent to all the Catholic dogmas. On the other hand, I meet acknowledged Catholics who do not take seriously the canonical conditions for members and who sometimes believe fewer Catholic dogmas than I do. Moreover, I am openly made welcome as a communicating fellow Catholic by Catholic groups and individuals. What criteria should I use to decide my possible Catholic identity?[11]

It might seem that in the more conservative nineties churches will find people seeking greater control over membership and belief and stronger ties of belonging. Certainly there is some evidence that leaders – vicars and ministers – are pressing, or responding to pressure, for this. Baptismal discipline, for example, is a notable point of contemporary anxiety, especially in the Church of England. But the most important factor in this change may prove to lie elsewhere.

Whatever else this era may be, it is indubitably that of the lay person. In every period of history people have probably picked and chosen among the range of beliefs available to them. But, apart from some noted public dissenters, eclecticism has been a matter of private reservation in the setting of public conformity. Today in many areas of life there is a reassertion of the importance of the lay person, that is, someone with interest, ability and commitment but who is not part of a professional coterie of experts. In part this may be the public flowering of the idea of personal authority, which has derived from the long period of post-Enlightenment emphasis on individual autonomy. At another level it is perhaps less an affirmation of 'lay' as such than a stance adopted against the apparent privileges of the expert. In religion, politics and medicine the modern lay person believes largely what he or she is willing to accept and seeks sufficient association rather than intense belonging in the sense of holding all that has been and is taught.[12] If this is genuinely so, it seems likely that the greater the emphasis on commitment to the local church the more some people will correspondingly seek personally enlarging experiences elsewhere. Again, we are confronted with a problematic situation for pastors: the greater their success at establishing the local congregation (as they are required to do today in most churches, whatever their formal polity), the more their people are going to turn from them for inspiration and teaching.

There is another pressure towards simplicity, even naivety, amid the welter of beliefs and practices that will surround and be found within the Church during this decade. The complexities of life are becoming such that convolutions of belief are felt by many to be an added (even unnecessary) burden rather than a result of engagement with issues that matter. All contemporary churches display fundamentalist trends, which are more than technical biblical fundamentalism. For example, we may discern an ecclesiological fundamentalism, which closes discussion about the ordering of the church, whether by insistence on episcopacy, for instance, or the rights of synodical representation. Either way new authoritarian styles of behaviour emerge. Sacramental fundamentalism is the sustaining mark of parts of the church, leading to the protection of the Eucharist or exclusive baptismal disciplines. Liberal fundamentalism, although possibly now in retreat, is still to be found, with its tendency towards intolerance. Adherents of each of these perspectives, which are not mutually exclusive, claim that their stance offers a direct solution to the dilemmas of contemporary belief. In this way they escape the complexity and disorienting experience of faith that arises from dialogue between these different perspectives. Although some still stand firmly for such interaction, it seems that for many the quick and direct solution to what is insoluble may become even more attractive.

One factor which contributes to this pressure towards simplicity is the uncertainty generated by intractable ethical issues. Humankind seems to be standing on a threshold. In matters to do with the human self and the body awesome prospects are opening up, which may be for either good or ill. Questions of personal identity and value are increasingly intertwined and no member of a single profession – scientist, priest, philosopher or lawyer – is able to address them with sufficient competence to convey conviction.

The Christian tradition remains rich in resources for facing such issues. It is clear, however, that this resource is not applicable in the modern world without a great deal of cool-headed thinking and imaginative reflection. This is a risky enterprise, since making a mistake today is regarded as unforgivable and therefore inadvisable. When those in positions to make such mistakes are themselves often unwilling or unable to acknowledge any authority beyond their own, a sense of disaster looms whenever any new discovery or prospect emerges.

These issues, and more, add up to the basic topics to be faced in the coming decade. Are people, then, beginning to acknowledge that there is some kind of spiritual void? If so, how might and should the Christian churches respond? And even if the churches falter, does the Christian faith still possess the resources and capacity to speak to contemporary people? In other words, is the gospel true?

Conclusion

These questions comprise today's context for Christian churches. They are also topics around which the phenomenon of the New Age coalesces. This may prove to be an ephemeral efflorescence of religiosity at the end of a millennium and be scarcely worth attention. But historically minded Christians, who note parallels between New Age and second-century gnostic thinking, will also recall that the fact of Gnosticism (even more than the detailed content of belief) had a profound impact on the way that the Church developed and the gospel was formulated. So even if the New Age phenomenon fails to survive long after the turn of the millennium, the questions raised by the religious and cultural context in which the Church is now set, and which are given priority by the New Age, remain to be addressed. One advantage to Christian ministers of considering the New Age phenomenon is that it encourages them to articulate these vast issues in relation to alternative views which are Western based but which are not defined by the Church.

Although the New Age has no formal structure, its expression is now sufficiently coherent for us to consider it as an entity. It is a mélange of beliefs and attitudes, but is marked by similar tendencies to those which can be noted in the churches. There is, for example, a tendency to reject order and structure, especially formal religious systems. Each belief or position is held with a conscious awareness of a wide range of associations, which may or may not be accepted, as the believer wishes. And scientific achievements are acknowledged, coupled with the recognition that these are ambiguous. In thinking about the context of the last decade of the millennium, therefore, the phenomenon of the New Age presents a point of interpretative comparison with what the churches' ministers are seeking to do and believe.

Looking at this relationship in reverse, the New Age attitude to Christianity is equivocal. Writers frequently imply, and sometimes claim, that Christianity as a religion is a spent force. Other New Agers, however, continue to affirm that much spiritual value remains in Christianity but that it needs rescuing from the dross of the residual faith. The danger for the churches in this ambiguity is obvious. On the one hand, the Church like any institution needs enemies, real or imagined, in order to define itself. The New Age phenomenon can be today's convenient enemy, not least since in many respects the way it is emerging looks not too dissimilar from the early history of the Church. On the other hand, there is a danger of an eclectic response producing a sort of syncretism against which the Christian Church has always set itself. These problems are illustrated, for example, in the work of Matthew Fox, a Roman Catholic priest; the activities at St James', Piccadilly, an Anglican church; the Creation Centred Liturgies, which have been held at various cathedrals; and the use by New Age thinkers of the ideas of such significant but esoteric Christians as Teilhard de Chardin and Thomas Merton.

What follows is not an exposition of the New Age phenomenon. Such a task would, in practice, be difficult and probably useless because of the range of beliefs and activities which go under this heading and the rapid change to which all are subject. It would also be to attribute to something of doubtful intrinsic importance attention which it may not deserve and especially to impose upon it a structure which it would not yet claim. The issues which are indicated by the emergence of the New Age, however, are important. The following chapters, therefore, are an attempt to review these as they may affect the churches and their activities during the decade to the end of this millennium. They are addressed to thinking, working ministers, who in the end are the people who have to interpret what is going on in and around the Church.

NOTES

1 Eileen Barker. *New Religious Movements: A Practical Introduction* (London. HMSO. 1989).

2 'A Vision of Mandulis Aion', in *Essays on Religion and the Ancient World* (Oxford. OUP. 1972), vol. i, pp. 357ff.

3 See. for a recent exposition of this theme. Lesslie Newbigin. *The Gospel in a Pluralist Society* (London. SPCK. 1989).

4 Robin Gill. *Beyond Decline* (London. SCM. 1988). The classic debate may be found in David Martin. *A General Theory of Secularization* (Oxford, Blackwell. 1978); and Brian Wilson. *Religion in Secular Society* (London. Penguin. 1969). On the media see in general Wesley Carr. *Ministry and the Media* (London. SPCK. 1990); and on the US electronic church. Stewart Hoover. *Mass Media Religion: The Social Sources of the Electronic Church* (London. Sage. 1988).

5 Bryan Wilson's description of the simultaneously radical and conservative stance of sectarian behaviour accords well with the experience of many in today's Church of England:

> [Sects] are radical in the challenge that they pose to constituted religious authority; they reject the procedures and activities of the dominant church . . . ; they dissociate themselves from many aspects of the secular culture . . . On the other hand. they are conservative in that they often seek to re-assert moral and religious precepts which they see as having become neglected in the dominant tradition . . . They condemn contemporary authority either for failing to maintain original religious ideals. or sometimes for failing to accept new revelation. *Religion in a Sociological Perspective* (Oxford, OUP. 1982), pp. 105f.

6 David Edwards. *The Futures of Christianity* (London. Hodder & Stoughton. 1987), p. 448.

7 See Wesley Carr, *The Priestlike Task* (London. SPCK. 1985).

8 This attitude reached its apotheosis in John Tiller. *A Strategy for the Church's Ministry* (London. CIO. 1983).

9 Charles Handy. *The Age of Unreason* (London. Business Books. 1989).

10 See Grace Davie. 'Believing without Belonging. Is this the future of religion in Britain?', *Social Compass* 37 (1990), pp. 455ff.

11 Charles Davis. 'Our New Religious Identity'. cited by John Robinson. *Where Three Ways Meet* (London. SCM. 1987). p. 122.

12 Hugh Dawes. 'Liberal Theology in the Parish'. *Theology* (1990), pp. 117ff.

2 | A New Age?

The idea of the New Age is worth the Church's attention, not least because it represents a lively response to the demands of the context in which ministry has to be exercised to the year 2000. In particular, the phenomenon indicates something about people, their sense of self and the way in which their experience is interpreted. Most New Age material claims to return to forgotten dimensions of basic human experience and to recover lost interpretations (usually religious). Such coherence as this amalgam of ideas possesses first emerged in the western United States. As a phenomenon the New Age is an instance of a movement which is familiar in European and Western history: the westward thrust of invasion and migration pushes unabsorbed aspects of culture and life before it, until the sea is reached. There they can go no further, stop, often ossify, but do not disappear. We can see this progression in legends from and about Cornwall, Wales, Ireland, the New World, the Wild West and eventually California. When the Pacific is reached, the West becomes as it were 'East' and Eastern influence is welcomed. But the core myth remains that to the West lies the repository of lost wisdoms and that from it a new leader or movement will arise.

There is, however, no 'new age'. Sometimes the phrase is used as if it stood for a single phenomenon, possibly even an embryonic new religious organization.[1] But that assumption is erroneous. We are dealing with something less defined or ordered. It is consequently difficult to consider. On the one hand, if we are too specific, we assign the New Age a status which its adherents do not acknowledge and thus misinterpret it; on the other hand, if we are too general we are in danger of underestimating its potential and influence on people.

New Age is best regarded as an unstructured network of attitudes and beliefs. In the following pages the word 'network' will often be used. It is, however, important not to conceive even this too systematically. The essence of the phenomenon is its unstructured nature. These beliefs and attitudes connect with one another, often in unexpected ways, to generate not just a revolution but, it is hoped, a new form of change – 'The Aquarian conspiracy'. The reference is astrological: the tired age of Pisces, the Fish (which roughly equates with the period of Judaeo-Christian dominance) is giving way to that of Aquarius, the Water-carrier. That which is now dry will flourish with new vitality as he brings living water and what is now becoming soulless desert will once again turn green. The transformation is to be total: it will both affect individual attitudes and involve social change. As personal consciousness is awakened and raised, social transformation will be accomplished.

It is not possible to be certain exactly what is included within the network and what, if anything, is excluded. The complications of connectedness are many and under the umbrella 'new age' we find, for example, such an incongruous mix as human potential movements, astrology, witchcraft (usually white), sometimes Satanism, ecological concerns, channelling of spirits from the beyond, and fascination with Unidentified Flying Objects (UFOs). A network of this type necessarily has no organization, but some key pointers or centres around which this way of thinking coalesces can be discerned.

It often adopts current scientific ideas and attitudes. These, however, are separated from what are regarded as their sterile rationalistic consequences, which are believed to have contributed to the creation of the modern world. From these constraints human beings need to be freed. Of interest to Christians, for example, is the prominence given to Teilhard de Chardin, about whose synthesis of palaeon-tology and theology neither scientists nor theologians are sure. Another example is found in the World Wide Fund for Nature and its religious advisers, the International Consultancy on Religion, Education and Culture (ICOREC), which link personal belief (often religious) with scientifically-based action. There is a proliferation of New Age occasional literature, lists and journals which sustain connections between individuals and groups. Shops, too, such as Compendium and the Alternative Bookshop, are natural places of association. Communities are also important, both as places to go and as ideals to admire. In the UK the most famous New Age centre was at Findhorn in Scotland, but many others regularly advertise. Some parts of the network assume a specifically religious form, such as in the Aetherius Society, which has its own ecclesial order, including bishops. Public festivals are significant, the best known in the UK being the annual festival of Mind–Body–Spirit.

But even such a loose and wide-ranging set of connections cannot be easily identified as 'the New Age'. In the nature of the case some group or other will object to their being ordered in a particular fashion. Under this all-embracing phrase, however, four themes recur.

First, creation and nature are central. As with much popular ecology, there is a sense that the human species has reached the end of the line in abusing the planet, which may be striking back in a quasi-personal way. The Gaia hypothesis that the earth is self-sustaining through a process of dynamic feedback, frequently overlaid with deliberate anthropomorphism, continues to have mystical influence.[2] Second, the attitude adopted towards the world and people is holistic. Ideas about the new physics are joined to older types of religious or humanitarian holism. Talk about quantum theory and Buddhism is thus possible in the same breath. New Age and modern scientific theory are brought together, although the proponents of New Age reflection fear that dimensions significant both for nature and for the human spirit have been lost in the growth of a scientific and secularized society. This perception leads, thirdly, to a willingness to welcome rather than discount the irrational side to human behaviour, including those superstitions which have been on the whole derided during this century. But lastly, underlying all of this, is an interest in power and its exercise. That energy may be untapped human potential, the latent forces in nature, the controls of witchcraft, the domination of the stars, or spiritual powers. But whatever the format, New Age thinking addresses people's anxiety about control, especially the fundamental question of whether we are ultimately in control of our destinies or whether they control us.

Each of these themes can be found in most of the literature. Separately they are of little specific interest. They can be found at almost any period of human history, and one of the problems of dealing with some of the material is its uncritical appeal to historical precedent. The distinctive mark of the New Age approach is the way in which it sets out to bring ideas and stances into conjunction, in order to produce a synthesis which resists analysis and cumulatively has many attractions. The process of reaching synthesis and the claim that it can be legitimately achieved is for many more attractive than either the component parts or the resulting production. It is important to grasp that the ideal of integration is the guiding factor. Devotion to this allows people to acknowledge parts of the mixture of ideas with which they themselves are not necessarily in sympathy.

This may best be seen in an example. The following mixture of process and content is taken from a small broadsheet which was produced in Bristol by Freeze/The Safer World Project. It is typical of many such publications, cheaply produced, with a limited circulation, but fired with zeal. The article was written as a response to the report by the General Synod of the Church of England's Board of Social Responsibility, *Peacemaking in a Nuclear Age*.

The Report considers the Christian concepts of Pax, Shalom and Inner Peace. We also need a concept of peace which shows how we have to be in harmony with nature, as well as harmony with our fellow beings. The realisation of our dependence on the natural world is not particularly emphasised in Christian teaching, and insufficiently appreciated by an increasingly urbanised and industrialised society. In an interdependent world we should draw more on the experience of the Eastern religions. Also we might learn from peoples who, though less economically and technically advanced than ourselves, nevertheless have a profound understanding of their position as part of nature rather than masters of it. One is not advocating a return to 'primitive' or overly simple lifestyle but to one which shows greater understanding of the ecological dimension in peacemaking. As a result of our desire to dominate and control, we find ourselves threatened by a choice of two ways to experience an untimely end – either by a planned or accidental nuclear disaster or by a less dramatic, but equally possible, collapse of the ecosystem, with the pollution and degradation of air, soil and water. All the biological sciences stress the need to conserve and to protect the environment. Any analysis of peacemaking that does not recognise this dimension, as part of long-term security, is inadequate.[3]

While not from a 'formal' New Age publication, this quotation illustrates the hallmarks of this stance. The basic attitude is holistic, as the writer tries to bring all things into some unity. She demonstrates her concern with nature and creation. While acknowledging the significance of science, she sets aside Christianity (mentioning it but presenting it as inadequate by setting it in a context of an 'increasingly industrial and urbanised society'). The idea of interdependence is promoted through Eastern religions, which are assumed to be implicitly more mystical than Judaism or Christianity and hence able to cope with the irrational. It is in this local, almost domesticated form, that most ministers are likely first to encounter the New Age. Odd moments when its pervasiveness emerges are more common than massive ordered presentations of an alternative religious movement.

New Age as a response to a distinctive context

World views are not dreamed up: they emerge within but also as contributors to specific contexts. Hannah Arendt has somewhere suggested that we owe modern secularizing trends to the invention of the telescope. When people were able to view their familiar world through this instrument, their perception of it was so altered that they had themselves to undergo such a profound adjustment in their thinking and conceptualizing that a whole new process of thought was inaugurated. The old world had been lost and a new one had to emerge. Some suggest further that this is one step among many in human development, which begins from the first sense of the Self and the Other and is sustained through life by the existence of mirrors in which the Self is perceived as Other.[4]

The claims made for the New Age are not dissimilar. Whatever their intrinsic credibility, they direct attention not only to themselves but to the context in which they arise. Christian theologians eventually had to come to terms with the telescope. They discovered that they could not confound the empiricism of Galileo's successors simply through a literal reading of Acts 1.11, 'Why do you stand looking into heaven?'[5] In so doing they began to come to terms with the emerging secular viewpoints. Their activities and thinking were radically affected and in time adjusted.

It would be excessive to compare the potential change which may result from New Age thinking with that which followed Galileo's invention, although some New Agers argue that a change on a similar scale – a 'paradigm shift' – will occur.[6] But a synthesis of ancient lore and new science to create a sense of present awe and mystery seems attractive to some serious thinkers and artists of the day. The options of being 'purely' scientific or 'purely' theological are declining. The new physics, especially quantum theory and cosmology, as well as the Chaos hypothesis, encourage a sense of synthesis.[7] Christian ministers need to consider not only these new ideas, obscure as they frequently are, but also the context which they are creating for the expression of religious ideas. Why does a wide-ranging network of felt association around nebulous ideas hold such attraction? What can be the connection between ufology[8] and Satanism or between Jungian psychology and campaigns for saving the whales?

(a) The new perspective. The word 'context' is vague, but a more secure grasp of the idea may be gained through examining it in terms of boundaries. The New Agers propose that the old boundaries which gave order to individual (what makes the Self) and to social life (what makes culture possible) have become constraints. For example, religion provided the sense of ultimate boundaries to life and death and so helped people regulate their relationships between the cradle and the grave. More recently psychological theories have weakened people's sense of the boundaries that define them, not least by complicating our sense of self. As a result they now seem to destroy rather than sustain both the human spirit and its environment. The claim is thus made that the old religions are tired and no longer effective and that orthodox medicine and psychiatry need to be replaced by holistic medicine and human potential. The boundary, too, between *homo sapiens* and the animal and vegetable world needs softening, through a deeper sense of human unity with nature and the practice of vegetarianism. And even the normal confines of time and space can be overcome, either by mystical activities with crystals and other ancient lore or by space travel, real (as to the moon) or imaginary (as with UFOs).

Intrinsic to this style of thinking, therefore, is the ambivalence which results from our going beyond what we know. On the one hand, the excitement of naughtiness accompanies exploration of what was hitherto forbidden. On the other hand, there is fear, since who knows what dangers lurk unforeseen? Anxiety is reduced, however, when such hazards are safely identified with what is believed really to be known but temporarily forgotten – the old ways. The phrase 'New Age', therefore, is misleading. What is 'new' is the future. The ways of facing it are as much old as new. For example, the theory of quantum physics, which is clearly 'new', may be used to recover lost dimensions of life – its interactive nature and the way in which one small facet may contain the whole – which are very 'old'.

The scientific argument is based on the new perspectives that we as human beings are discovering on ourselves and our place in the universe. We have moved physically outwards and are the first humans to observe the planet Earth as an object hanging in space. The experience is one of extraordinary beauty, which draws attention to Earth's comparative insignificance in the universe. This vision matches the new theories of cosmologists. The aesthetic experience and the theories combine to make us aware of the fragility of our planet and ourselves and of the delicacy of the balance which enables anything to survive.

In the other direction, towards the interior, the work of geneticists and microbiologists demonstrates on what small differences the infinite variegatedness of human beings relies. And in a curious fashion, the more the beauties of the micro-world of genes, DNA and the like are exposed to us, the more congruent they appear to be with the vast galaxies of space. This is an era for drawing parallels and seeking unifying theories. Indeed the holy grail of the decade might be a unified field theory.[9]

New Age thinking is in part a response to these disturbances about the boundaries of human existence. It tries to integrate the social, religious, psychological and spiritual dimensions, because, so it appears, none are secure and no one, and certainly no church, can any longer speak with authority about them. The story of Edgar Mitchell is an intriguing example of how such feelings may be aroused and of a reaction to them. Mitchell flew one of the NASA missions to the moon. The experience had a profound effect on him. He writes:

The presence of divinity* became almost palpable and I *knew* that life in the universe was not just an accident based on random process . . . My wonderment gradually turned to something close to anguish, because I realized that at the very moment when I was so privileged to view the planet from 240,000 miles in space, people on Earth were fighting wars: committing murder and other crimes: lying, cheating and struggling for power and status: abusing the environment by polluting the water and air, wasting natural resources and ravaging the land, acting out of lust and greed: and hurting others through intolerance, bigotry, prejudice, and all the things that add up to man's inhumanity to man.[10]

Mitchell subsequently founded The Institute of Noetic Sciences, where he attempts to bring together Eastern mystics and leaders in Western computer science. His personal fame attracts business people and others to study there. The message is that somewhere within human beings lies the potential to save themselves from all those disastrous mistakes and behaviour on which he meditated in his space capsule. The new perspective is thus intended to lead to new behaviour and so usher in a new age.

(b) Psychology. Late twentieth-century Westerners live in a post-Freudian age. The technical disputes over psycho-analysis continue. But from the pioneering work of Freud, Jung, Adler and others a widespread acknowledgement of the unconscious mind and its influence on people's behaviour has emerged. Some basic tenets have become part of an everyday language of interpretation. In particular they have influenced the way in which relationships and roles are understood. They have had a major impact on such institutions as the family and on the work of people like teachers, social workers, doctors, judges and, not least,

---

*Note that he says 'divinity' and not 'a divinity', an important distinction for some New Agers.

clergy. Much is now taken for granted from the study of human behaviour, both conscious and unconscious.

One paradoxical outcome, however, seems to be greater confusion about the individual self and his or her personal identity. Each of the three classic discoveries of Freud, his colleagues and successors, contributes. The idea of the unconscious mind is easy to grasp. Few people are unfamiliar with dreaming. The notion, therefore, that somewhere within the mind there is another dimension which has, as it were, a life of its own, can be grasped. Since dreams can often be remembered and so reflected upon, it is a simple step to recognize that this unconscious world is in some circumstances accessible to our consciousness. The second theme, transference, is the source of many jokes about analysts and their patients. The individual treats another as if he or she were someone else of significance in their life history. While the focus of attention in analytic process, this is not the prerogative of the trained but a basic phenomenon of everyday life. Thirdly, projection describes the way in which individuals dispose of parts of themselves that they find uncomfortable or distasteful into another person and respond to them in him or her.

These discoveries became possible because of assumptions about individual autonomy. To some extent modern psychology has also been taken to affirm these. But as the end of the century approaches Westerners are becoming increasingly aware of other possible consequences of this autonomy. Is the price of affirmed individual autonomy disregard for others? Does self-awareness inevitably produce selfishness that shows itself in acquisitiveness or aggression – taking things from others or doing things to them? The world view which takes human beings as autonomous individuals, who may stand outside and observe themselves and others, also has an impact. And discoveries in psychology generate further uncertainty about what or who the so-called autonomous individual is.

This topic might be more explorable if it were not simultaneously compounded by new findings in biology. We are uncertain what individuals are in relation to their inner lives: we are unsure about how to relate to others: and now we cannot even decide when the individual is to be recognized as a biological entity. Research in psychobiology, especially how a person might be manipulated by drugs and other therapies, makes the solution to the question of identity seem even further distant. The philosopher William James may well have been more right than he knew in 1892, when he suggested that since the 'I' would be elusive it might better be left to philosophers than to empirical psychologists.[11]

These difficulties with the concept of individuality are complicated by confusions at the social level. One mark of Western societies, which in 1990 was dramatically confirmed in Eastern Europe, is the loss of confidence in familiar institutions. The established points, the boundary markers, in our society appear less reliable and fewer people seem willing or able to risk relying on them. These signs may be institutions which have hitherto been regarded as fundamental, such as church, school, family, or monarchy and parliament. Or they may be norms of behaviour, such as the way the people of different gender relate to one another. The same seems true for the less obvious securities of life, especially the continuance of companies and other organizations and consequently their role in giving people a sense of their place in the world. If we turn inwards, confident at least in our own autonomy, we find that this inner world has itself become a challenge to any certainty. If we look outwards to others and to the institutions of our societies, we cannot identify secure places by which to orient ourselves in an increasingly boundaryless world.[12]

One response to these dilemmas has been to emphasize human potential. This takes various forms, but essentially all focus around a few points. Behavioural studies are treated as sciences, but they are reckoned to have ignored a dimension of the self. We each, so the argument runs, have hidden inner resources which, if they can be tapped, can transform the self and our relations to others. These ideas are expressed in popular psychological writing, which in many ways is like wisdom writing, whether Judaeo-Christian or other. It consists of a set of aphorisms and directions which, if followed, should bring some sort of happiness. The approach then drifts into connections with parapsychology. These attitudes are commonplace today. The human potential material, however, has been distinctively taken as a central theme for the New Age.

The field of human potential offers clear instances of networking and the way that ideas drift into haphazard association. On the one hand, and most dangerously, anxiety may lead people to surrender themselves to the control of others. They find themselves manipulated by quasi-cultic techniques of persuasion and control. On the other hand, the same starting points can lead to occultism. This is a sort of psychic technology, whereby the ancient wisdoms and lore (often presented as such without historical justification) are given the respectability of a modern 'rationale'. Magic, occultism, parapsychology and popular self-help coincide under the guise of human potential. This theme in turn connects with three familiar dimensions of New Age, which, however, not all who would associate with the title would accept.

First, there is a preoccupation with the strange and unexplained. For example, encounters with extra-terrestrial beings and observing flying saucers have played a part in the movement, chiefly in the USA. The longing to be able to demonstrate that there are dimensions within this world, the origins of which actually lie beyond it, is strong. Science fiction is widely read, not just by those associated with New Age. The work of, for instance, Arthur C. Clarke has a seminal influence.[13] Natural fascination with things which appear abnormal is elevated to the status of significant enquiry, without, however, surrender to the notion that a scientific (in other words 'sceptical') approach would be appropriate.

Second, there is a search for hidden connections between events. Exploration of coincidence follows the lines of, for example, Arthur Koestler's *The Roots of Coincidence*.[14] Such believed connections are explored by some through record keeping and parapsychological research but by others through magic. The Tarot cards, for example, are important. A New Age Aquarian set, the characters on which are claimed to have been revealed through a session of guidance through a ouija board, is popular.

These two areas – fascination with anomalies and connections – spill over into the third dimension, where they are formalized in various belief systems. The Wicca, or witchcraft, is one such example, which gives particular attention to femaleness and the place of women. It is possible, although the topic is obscure, that Satanism might be another such theme. Benign influences might be found at places of mystery, such as Stonehenge, or in unexplained ideas such as that of the ley-lines or belief in corn-circles.

The general description for these beliefs might best be neo-pagan, the rediscovery of forms of belief which are believed to have predated the Christian era. Obliterated, but never wholly destroyed by the dominance of the Christian Church, they are claimed to be returning to their rightful place in human life.

(c) The century of violence. New perspectives on ourselves and our past do not arise in a cultural and social vacuum. If today we look for one field of human experience which is common to every person in the Western world, we do not have to look far. Everyone, whatever their age, has lived through a period of continuous aggression. Wars have dominated the twentieth century. My own life is not untypical: born during the Second World War; aware of war in the Far East and Korea; facing, but just missing, National Service and the wars in Malaya, Cyprus and the Middle East; as a student very conscious of the Cold War and subsequently affected by Vietnam; constantly made aware of lesser skirmishes, until the reality of the Falklands campaign; and then completing the final draft of this book between the prospect and outbreak of war in Kuwait in

1991. Experiences in war do not affect those directly involved alone: they also influence subsequent generations. But there is a second factor – the prevalence of the media. These present past wars to subsequent generations through war stories, films or humour. But the effect is the same: the war is relived. The news media also bring reports of wars directly into people's homes. These may be of combat in which the viewing nation is directly involved or of wars that seem personally distant. But there is no escape for anyone from wars.

This observation links with another area of aggression, which characterizes contemporary life: the belligerence which marks urban living. It is easy to generalize about this, but the reasons for it defy explanation. 'Mindless' violence is nothing new and its history has been studied. But because it is a convenient focus, it seems to be used sometimes to obscure the ubiquitous 'war model' of everyday life. For there are fights against drugs and struggles for success. Life is now openly competitive. Trade is less a matter of mutual agreement by striking bargains than a fight which is won or lost. Every occasion is one for potential conflict and the belief is sustained that only through militancy can anything be achieved.

Christopher Lasch suggests that the underlying issue is one of survival, which has been crystallized in this century by the Holocaust.

> An early study of the death camps announced in its title the question that has continued to absorb the late twentieth-century imagination: 'how did they survive?' . . . It is a question that runs through all our thinking about the Nazi death camps: but it also runs through historical investigations of other minorities subjected to persecution and discrimination, through the psychiatric literature on stress and 'coping mechanisms', and through much of the popular writing on stresses experienced in the business world . . . Adversity takes on new meanings in a world

where the concentration camp stands as a compelling metaphor for society as a whole. Competition, for example, now centers not so much on the desire to excel as on the struggle to avoid a crushing defeat.[15]

Survival is, however, not just a social or national issue; it also concerns the individual. A survival-oriented narcissism[16] seems to produce among its effects family conflict and the consequential damage to children, which in turn replicates itself in subsequent generations. The outcome of all this struggle, both in wars, life and the individual, is a pervasive war weariness. This may manifest itself in the wish to escape world conflict, family dissension, inter-personal friction or even merely tussles within the self.

Such longings have historical precedents, although in each generation the form of the expectation is culturally conditioned. As this century comes to an end the desire for relief is confused by two factors. First, there is the history of war and aggression. It seems inescapable, since wherever we turn the violence is found. There is no avoiding it by either going to another place or looking forward to another time. Secondly, there is a new factor – namely the number of people involved. Numbers in conflicts become so large as to be incomprehensible. It began in the First World War when millions died: it was confirmed at Hiroshima and Nagasaki and in the later nuclear debates about Mutually Assured Destruction. And other struggles, such as those around famine and disease in the Third World, repeat it. The size of populations and the numbers involved in the struggle for survival seem to emphasize in people's minds the sense of 'us' and 'them' and produce opposing resonances which parallel the actual war and aggression. There is, therefore, both the hope for peace and security and a strong sense that because survival is so high on the human agenda, this ideal cannot be achieved.

If we were to seek one point of almost complete agreement among New Agers, concern for peace in its widest sense would probably prove such a unifying focus. The literature is suffused with the longing for harmony and order in a world which feels increasingly alien. This hope is sometimes expressed in terms of evolutionary progression and human development. The human species is maturing and should be able to discard its tendency to fight. One way would be the abandonment of nationalism. The world is becoming a smaller place and the hope for peaceful coexistence through global government sustains many. The parallel stance is a rejection of every nostrum which has demonstrably failed, whether these be old nations, old forms of government or the old religions, including Christianity.

The holistic tendency of the New Age appears around issues of peace. It holds three dimensions together. First, there is that inner peace which can come from religious or quasi-religious experience. The human potential movement, mysticism and pagan religions offer their various solaces. But, secondly, a commitment to and desire for world peace between people and nations and tribes is also required. Here the urge is towards ideals of universal culture and the loss of differences. Much New Age literature, however, goes further and, thirdly, links inner and world reconciliation to the concept of peace as itself divine or coming from a divine source. It is important, however, to notice that 'divine' does not necessarily mean 'from God'. The concept of divinity is not that formalized and this looseness allows multiple interpretations. Such openness is conducive to easier association between like-minded people. Peace, then, is a complex idea generated by fusing inner peace, world peace and divine peace, each informing and being informed by the other.

(d) Astrology. This subject also has an astrological dimension, which is sometimes, though not always, explicit. The age of Pisces (the Fish) is approximately that of the Judaeo-Christian era. The predominant culture of this period has been described as one of 'creative selfishness', in which individuals and groups, including churches, pursue their self-interest but, in so doing, prove creative. Hence we inherit

the remarkable cultural achievements of that era. These, however, have only been realized at considerable cost and damage to others, because of the assumption of competition and struggle. This age is now giving place to the age of Aquarius (the Water-carrier), which is marked by balance and order. There will also specifically be a decline of Christian influence, which will lead to more harmony.

The theme of the Age of Aquarius was introduced in the late 1960s through the song of that title in the musical *Hair*. That presented ideas which have subsequently been elaborated in New Age astrological writing. As with all astrology dates are less certain than we might expect. But roughly the theory proposes a two-stage transformation of the world. The first is the period between 1846 and 1918, when the rise of the two great empires of the USA and USSR begins. The second phase is from 1918 to about 1990, when something will end. At the time of most of this writing it is unclear what this could be. By 2062, however, the transformation will be complete and the Age of Aquarius will have dawned.[17]

Ideas which have customarily been associated with astrology or expressed through it are prevalent in New Age thinking. We need, however, to clarify the idea of astrology, otherwise we may fail to appreciate the power of its attraction for many. Those not involved tend to treat all astrological activity as if it were something to do with horoscopes. Astrology, however, consists of two main types. On the one hand, there is universal astrology, which tends to be fatalistic. The immutable movements of the stars and planets direct events in a way which might be discovered but about which it may even be best not to know. This is the astrology of the thinking person: whatever people do, the heavens seem destined to win. On the other hand, there is today's more popular notion of the individual astrology of the horoscope. The division is an ancient one:

Human nature being what it is, the harsh principle of fatalistic astrology was appealing to the sober, scientific minded minority only. Most of those who believed in astrology at all preferred the catarchic doctrine, permitting man to 'outsmart' the heavens. As for the masses, star worship and catarchic* astrology with them remained popular at all times from the hellenistic era to the end of paganism in the Roman empire.[18]

Such behaviour is religious: it represents a search for salvation either from or through the overwhelming powers which seem to govern our destinies. The theory of the Age of Aquarius appears to have many of the marks of universal astrology, with its talk of the fatalistic rise and fall of empires and religions. In practice, however, as with most astrological procedures in history, it shifts towards being catarchic. Whatever the fate of empires, it takes a very cold and rational person to consider these without asking the personal question: How can I (or we) achieve the power to control our fate? In the ancient world, for example, only a few Stoics seem to have managed it. It is unlikely that people have changed that much in the twentieth century.

(e) Knowledge and anxiety. The fourth contributing factor to the emergence of the New Age phenomenon is the way in which increased knowledge engenders anxiety. This is another ancient religious issue. The scientific knowledge which has been acquired over the last two centuries or so seems to be producing terminal anxiety in the world. The end of the Western belief in progress looks as though it might be the catastrophe of our own destruction. Things are so serious that even the nuclear threat, which has overshadowed the lives of so many in the past two generations, now seems to be relegated to the sidelines. The potential collapse of the ecosystem which sustains all life, through the decay of the ozone layer or the greenhouse effect, has assumed greater prominence. And, should men

---

catarchic: a technical word in ancient astrology which describes the reading of the stars to forecast events.

and women begin to feel that these dilemmas are possibly more manageable than had hitherto been thought, genetic engineering emerges to terrify people with the prospect of control over the nature of life itself. In whichever direction we look, anxiety is the companion of knowledge.

In the face of such disturbance, we might expect the New Age to turn back to pre-scientific ideas. But the response is generally not to discount modern knowledge in favour of primitive ignorance. Some may give that impression. But there are also those who seek a new sort of knowledge and promulgate a different science. This offers ways of bridging the mistakes of this age and connecting the past and the future in a creative fusion.

The first belief is that past knowledge which was of great value has been at worst systematically destroyed and at best just lost. At this point the New Age connects with the old religions. A simplistic view of history suggests that ancient lore and beneficial paganism have been extirpated by the ruthless dominating force of the Judaeo-Christian tradition, not least through the missionary character of Christianity. The old religions, mostly worshipping nature and in sympathy with it, represent an innocence which has been lost. At its more extreme form we find types of gnostic thinking, mostly dualistic in principle but being pressed as if they were holistic. There is a large amount of literature consisting of the recovery of hitherto lost texts of ancient wisdom or magic, some of which are genuine but many of which are imaginary.

The future orientation is found largely in the hope extended through the believed astrological control of destinies. That is one sort of knowledge. Alongside it stands another derived from the channelling of spirits. This technique is designed to bring the power of spirits, whether from another age or another world, to bear benignly on the lives of people, both those doing the invoking and the world in general. The similarity with astrology is obvious: the control of power from a source outside oneself marks both stances.

One example of thinking which attempts to integrate scientific discovery and ancient wisdom with future change is that based on the work of the Jesuit scientist and theologian, Pierre Teilhard de Chardin.[19] Controversial during his life, he remains so. From his palaeontological studies in China he developed a distinctive theological position. He regarded human beings as trapped in a 'bubble of the cosmos', where we fear both our and its ultimate demise. An evolutionary perspective, however, can enable us to see mankind's special history within the overall scheme of evolution and its potentially great future. Christ is perceived as both the origin and the goal of the cosmos. We are taken into the realm of hyperphysics, with the further suggestion that all matter possesses consciousness in either a rudimentary or developed form. The complex nature of the evolutionary process produces a rise of consciousness in matter which ultimately leads to the ascent of all things to consciousness.

This sketchy outline indicates why Teilhard de Chardin's work is important for the New Age. He himself was, because of the attitude of the church authorities, relegated to the margins of the Church. His studies preoccupied him at the edge of the world: China was culturally peripheral to the West. From his theory, however, it is possibly to deduce three strands of an argument.

First, the human spirit is a product of the evolution of many spirits. The integration of mankind with other forms of life and with matter itself is fundamental both to Teilhard's position and to that adopted by proponents of the New Age. This view, secondly, allows for the assumption that there are other spirits which may be evolving at other levels than our own. These may be 'below' us in the hierarchy and aspiring towards mankind's status. They may, however, possibly be 'above' us, more sophisticated and with a different and greater wisdom. Thirdly, once we conceive of this united hierarchy of spirit, it follows logically that the wish to communicate between the spirits is likely to be intrinsically part of what it means to be spirit.[20]

This brief excursion into the thought of Teilhard de Chardin in the context of the anxiety which is produced by knowledge is important. For in the New Age phenomenon it is crucial to have a concept of the value of matter and its preservation. This gives worth to the natural order and produces the associated 'green' attitudes. In addition, if there is a continuum from matter to spirit, it seems necessary to believe in something like reincarnation. All matter must somehow be preserved: there can be no genuine loss. Reincarnation is a way of dealing with this problem. However, in the West the idea of reincarnation has proved difficult to sustain. While we may suggest intellectually that this is a consequence of the dualisms which permeate Western thinking, it also remains the case that religions with schemes of reincarnation have not gained a hold. Hindu thought and Buddhist ideas may appear to be having greater influence in some quarters than hitherto. But even there the associated and varied reflections on reincarnation are not widely adopted.

Teilhard, however, apparently offers from within the Western scientific tradition a way of coming to terms with both continued existence after death and the wish to get in touch with the wisdom held there by other spirits, which may be recovered through channelling. What his views might have been had he known that his thinking could be used in this way must remain a mystery. But his thought is used to lend credibility to this activity.

Integrated living

Most people, not themselves especially interested in or aware of the New Age, are likely to meet adherents of it in connection with concern for the environment and holistic approaches to living. Neither of these positions can be considered fads or distinctive. The promotion of healthy diets and alternative life-styles, for instance, is central to health education. Indeed this stance is a primary form of contemporary puritanism. Christians have joined many others in urging upon people the need for simpler styles of living.[21] Third World crises have highlighted the inequalities in the system of world trade and dispersal of resources. The morality behind consumerism is widely questioned. No responsible citizen of a Western nation can now claim to be unaware of or unaffected by these concerns.

The New Age approach, however, incorporates and builds on these notions in a distinctive fashion. In it we may again observe the integrative style of thinking. The manifestations of simple living include vegetarianism, which both respects other 'higher' life forms and acknowledges the needs of other human beings; alternative technology, which builds into the idea of progress an express concern for the future environment; cottage industries, which endorse E. F. Schumacher's principle that 'small is beautiful'; and holistic living, which strives for harmony between the individual and his or her environment. These approaches, whether severally or together, make a statement about the nature of the world which we inhabit or, as their proponents would prefer to phrase it, with which we are integrated.

But that world is judged to be suffused with cosmic energy. As a result, what appear to be life-style decisions may also, if required, be seen as a means of tapping into that power. Parallel to this belief is the notion that the delinquent styles of living which most people have adopted produce a sickness both in the individual and in the land itself. The concept, therefore, of healing and therapy is also introduced. By the time these themes are put together, even something so simple as vegetarianism can become an indicator of a religious or therapeutic stance.

A means, however, has to be found to handle the obvious fact that human life and the world are not seamlessly interwoven. Experience indicates a discontinuity not a harmony. So a stance which is adopted at the level of personal life-styles has somehow to connect with the ways of viewing the world on a larger scale. We are again, therefore, introduced to aspects of contemporary scientific thinking about matter, space and time, such as are found in the Gaia hypothesis. Before this was articulated, others had viewed the earth as a living, interactive set of systems and spoken of it anthropomorphically. 'Gaia' – Earth – is more than a metaphor. She is not a way of viewing the earth but the earth *is* Gaia – a living, personal, female divinity, to be treated with an awe akin to worship. Although the hypothesis has been modified, the combination of scientific data, imaginative theory, respect for the feminine, implicit religion and earth mysticism is such that the thesis still carries weight. For many it also undergirds their attitude to environmental issues.

With this hypothesis we may connect two other contributory factors, both of which emanate less from quasireligious mysticism than from the new mysticism of modern science. First, there is Chaos theory. 'Where chaos begins, classical science stops . . . The irregular side of nature, the discontinuous and erratic side – these have been puzzles to science, or worse, monstrosities.'[22] This theory has been proposed as the third great scientific discovery of the century, alongside special relativity and quantum theory. Its central thrust is to discern and interpret connections between natural irregularities and apparently disconnected data, rather than as in classical science to construct ordering theories.

The second contributor is quantum physics. As theoretical and experimental physicists have pursued their researches in this century, a series of discoveries has ensued, which remain beyond the comprehension of most people. Two results are important and contribute in their popularized forms to the New Age thinking. The first, recently again proposed by Stephen Hawking, is that we may be reaching the end of an epoch in mankind's intellectual history as the prospect of achieving a unified field theory comes in sight.[23] But ending indicates not only achievement but also sterility. Having achieved ultimate understanding, we have nowhere further to go. Thus even in the modern world of scientific discovery, the old rules prevail: success is disappointing and urges the mind to seek new areas of discovery. Thus the greatest achievement, however original, remains part of an old order and proves that we are now at the dawning of a new age. At the theoretical level, the technicalities of modern cosmology are taken to authenticate the concept of the New Age as a new beginning.

The second result is less difficult for the lay person. The new physics seems to carry religious implications which are not derived from the theories but which reside within them. There is a confluence between those areas of life which are regarded as religious and those which have for nearly two centuries been separated as scientific. Ways of thinking about life, its purpose and meaning, and God fit naturally into discussions of the nature of the universe as these are pursued by the new physicists. For instance, a professor of theoretical physics ends a recent book with these words:

> I began by making the claim that science offers a surer path than religion in the search of [*sic*] God. It is my deep conviction that it is only by understanding the world in all its many aspects – reductionist and holist, mathematical and poetical, through forces, fields, and particles, as well as through good and evil – that we will come to understand ourselves and the meaning behind this universe, our home.[24]

More publications also use quantum theory as a basis for reflections upon the nature of consciousness and of human existence.[25] This provides for those who seek in it a further means of linking the microcosm of individual consciousness to the macro-structures of the universe.

At a less abstract level there remain the everyday questions of 'green' living. By comparison with the other ingredients of the New Age phenomenon these are difficult to assess, because they are the most politicized and most nearly have the characteristics of a movement. Green issues are high on the public agenda. The speed with which the term has become commonplace is evidence for this. They are also integral to the New Age phenomenon. However, in that setting they are never simple: we are always faced with an amalgam. The Wicca (witchcraft), for example, sees itself as green because it emphasizes the need to achieve harmony between people and nature. Peace, whether inner and personal or between parties and nations, leads to the idea that we need to discover peace in the battle between humankind and our environment, wherever that is found and however it is regarded.

These topics particularly confront the Christian Church through two approaches. First, there is a renewed emphasis on a creation-centred spirituality. Second, and linked with this, are the activities of the religious advisers to the World Wide Fund for Nature, the International Consultancy on Religion, Education and Culture. This makes explicit connections between green issues and religion through its promotion of creation-centred worship, sometimes of an inter-faith kind.

The feminine principle

One issue that has begun to emerge throughout the above discussion is the implicit importance of the feminine dimension to all of life. A strong commitment, sometimes as near as the New Age phenomenon gets to an ideology, is to the feminine principle. This is not specifically feminist. Definition of this notion, like that of the New Age, is disputed. Broadly speaking, however, we may say that feminism is a movement to overcome the oppression of women and discrimination against them. It especially attends to the social and cultural norms which embody this oppression. The idea of the feminine principle is less exact. It embraces a range of ideas which cumulatively direct attention to the belief that in every part of human life balance is needed between the intuitive and the rational, which are respectively regarded as the prerogative of the female and the male.

Equilibrium may be achieved through an affirmation of female spirituality, as in the case of the Wicca or worship of the Goddess. It sometimes finds expression in a longing for androgyny – the unification of opposites – as the ideal for human life. Overall, however, the argument is that two aspects of every individual – which are physiologically incorporated in the two hemispheres of the brain and socially manifest in the two sexes – have been unnecessarily and disastrously sundered. The rational ('male') dimension has dominated the intuitive and imaginative ('female') dimension, with a corresponding loss of cohesion in nature, society and the individual. The response is to give greater weight to the intuitive, the so-called 'feminine' principle. It is difficult to assess or argue this point. Whether we can describe the imaginative ideas which are found in the new physics, for instance, as feminine is not clear. The emphasis, however, overall is obvious: it is on connections and connectedness.

This is another key area where stances which are associated with the New Age calculatedly confront the Christian tradition. The Judaeo-Christian God is regarded as male – Father, with the powerfulness and dominance that have been attributed to the male in Western society. Since the corresponding subordination of women is reckoned to come to an end in the new climate, it is also assumed that its religious manifestation – the Judaeo-Christian God – is giving way to newer divinities. These might be the old religions of the Goddess in various guises. Alternatively the beliefs stress presumed feminine behaviour, such as sensitivity to aura and women's facility as mediums. The Age of Aquarius will allow the feminine principle to flourish. But since this is intrinsically inimical to the style of the exercise of power that males have hitherto displayed, it will not substitute for it but generate a new concept of power and a new fashion of its exercise will ensue.

We need to note two points here. First, as already mentioned, these ideas and stances do not constitute something peculiar to a phenomenon called 'The New Age'. These themes permeate Western societies and are being articulated in many places for a variety of reasons. But because of their pervasiveness, the New Age umbrella is one under which many of them connect. Secondly, within the sphere of the New Age some of these concepts emerge not purely for their own sake but because of the way that they combine with other dimensions. For instance, Wicca and belief in the Goddess join aspects of human potential, mysticism, ecology and nature and, most importantly, power and its exercise. They thus become important not solely for their specific contents but as a pattern which receives approbation for what it represents of the integrative hope of the New Agers. The area of feminine spirituality, feminism and religion is highly complex at present. It is part of a profound shift in society which it is too early to interpret with confidence.[26] As an area of New Age life and in its own right it carries questioning messages to the established religions.

Conclusion

This sketch of some of what passes under the heading 'New Age' and the contexts within which it arises, demonstrates that the New Age is a phenomenon and not a coherent body of belief. People with little in common in their attitudes, beliefs or behaviour may be lumped under the one head 'New Age'. It then becomes easy to dismiss both the whole and its parts as confused and confusing bits and pieces, which have been agglomerated into some sort of notional network.

That may be true, in which case there is no reason for Christian ministers to spend too much time on the detail of the New Age material. But to ignore it would also be a mistake. Many of the phenomena associated with New Age might make defensive Christians anxious or invite ridicule. But underlying these manifestations are topics which take us to the heart of religion in general and Christianity in particular, including what the Church will teach and practise in the next decade.

NOTES

1 This point is missed by some writers who, by treating the New Age as if it were an identifiable entity, give it a significance which it does not deserve. This then feeds their anxieties about a new religion. See, for instance, Michael Cole, Jim Graham, Tony Higton and David Lewis, *What is the New Age?* (London, Hodder & Stoughton, 1990); D. Groothius, *Unmasking the New Age* (Downers Grove, Illinois, Inter-Varsity Press, 1986).

2 James Lovelock, *Gaia: A New Look at Life on Earth* (Oxford, OUP, 1979).

3 Anula Beckett, *Towards a Safer World* (Bristol, Freeze, 1988). The author's permission to cite this passage is gratefully acknowledged.

4 See Morris Berman, *Coming to Our Senses: Body and Spirit in the Hidden History of the West* (London, Bantam, 1990), pp. 19ff.

5 See E. Haenchen, *The Acts of the Apostles* (Oxford, Blackwell, 1971, p. 150).

6 This is an example of the contemporary decay of language through imprecision. The phrase 'paradigm shift' is taken from Thomas Kuhn, *The Structure of Scientific Revolutions* (Chicago, UCP, 2nd edn 1969). Kuhn uses it to describe a rare but fundamental structural change in the way we think, a scientific revolution. The term has been popularized and is now used to describe any change that the proposer thinks might be radical.

7 An accessible introduction to the range of possible implications of the new physics is Paul Davies, *God and the New Physics* (Harmondsworth, Penguin, 1983). The popular book on chaos theory is James Gleick, *Chaos: Making a New Science* (London, Cardinal, 1988). Both contain extensive bibliographies.

8 'Ufology' is used to describe the pseudo-science of the study of Unidentified Flying Objects ('flying saucers') and engagements with extra-terrestrial beings.

9 See Davies, op. cit., pp. 155ff.

10 Edgar Mitchell, *Psychic Exploration* (New York, G. P. Putnam & Son, 1974).

11 From William James, *Psychology: The Briefer Course* (1892), cited by Berman, *Coming to Ourselves*, p. 348, n 38.

12 For an extended discussion of this issue see E. R. Shapiro and A. W. Carr, *Lost in Familiar Places* (New Haven, Yale University Press, 1991).

13 His novel and film *2001* is the most famous, but his *Childhood's End* is also popular.

14 London, Hutchinson, 1972.

15 Christopher Lasch, *The Minimal Self. Psychic Survival in Troubled Times* (London, Picador, 1985), p. 72.

16 Lasch also wrote *The Culture of Narcissism* (New York, Warner Books, 1979).

17 See, for instance, T. Roszak, *Unfinished Animal. The Aquarian Frontier and the Evolution of Consciousness* (London, Faber, 1976).

18 F. H. Cramer, *Astrology in Roman Law and Politics* (Philadelphia, 1954, p. 19).

19 In a small study conducted in 1977 in the USA, the most influential people mentioned were, in order of frequency, Teilhard de Chardin, Jung, Maslow, Rogers, Aldous Huxley, Assagioli and Krishnamurti. See Ferguson, *Aquarian Conspiracy*, pp. 460ff.

20 See, most accessibly, *The Phenomenon of Man* (London, Collins, 1959).

21 The Lifestyle Movement promoted by Horace Dammers is an instance. See his *An Alternative Lifestyle* (Wellingborough, Turnstone Press, 1982).

22 Gleick, *Chaos*, p. 3.

23 Stephen Hawking, *A Brief History of Time* (London, Bantam, 1988).

24 Davies, *God and the New Physics*, p. 229.

25 See, e.g., Danah Zohar, *The Quantum Self: A Revolutionary View of Human Nature and Consciousness Rooted in the New Physics* (London, Bloomsbury, 1990).

26 An excellent critical survey of the issues, which includes many helpful definitions, may be found in Ursula King, *Women and Spirituality: Voices of Protest and Promise* (London, Macmillan, 1989). See especially ch. 5, 'Voices of a new spirituality'.

3 | The Message of New Age to the Church

A mélange of ideas, such as those which are subsumed under the heading of 'New Age', is almost bound to include some points of which the Church should take notice. It can hardly miss. Three main issues, however, can be distilled as those to which ministers should especially give thought as they think about their ministry during this decade.

Eclecticism

The mass of New Age material is marked by two distinct attitudes. First, it is mainly uncritical. This is not the result of ignorance; many of the authors are highly educated, thinking people. The literature, therefore, does not represent a surge of anti-intellectualism. The disconcerting impact of their work arises because they are rejecting that analytical stance, which has been characteristic of Western thought since the Enlightenment, and adopting a synthetic way of arguing. There are signs that a sustained critique of contemporary intellectual assumptions may be beginning to emerge.

We might expect the learned world on the whole to be sceptical of this: that is its role. The churches, however, should recall that the Christian faith itself first provided the conditions for the emergence of such critical enquiry. In other words, this sort of intellectual and critical activity is itself integral to the Christian faith. At the intellectual level, therefore, the eclecticism of the New Age does not invite the response of a similar eclecticism from the churches. It addresses a more fundamental question at the heart of Christianity – What limits, if any, apply to the spirit of enquiry which the faith generates?

The approach, however, does sometimes become anti-critical. For it implies that the long history of Western achievement, which has been based upon the Judaeo-Christian religions, has produced an intellectual and emotional tradition which is no longer sustainable. The self-reflective stance – the ability to scrutinize oneself as object – is the foundation of contemporary enquiry. It is also the basis of that investment in therapy which is a present-day fashion. New Age thinking uses ideas of human potential which are based on this therapeutic model. But starting there it may tend towards becoming anti-critical as its holistic assumptions minimize, and often specifically obliterate, the subject/object distinction. This in turn changes perspectives not only on the mind and how thinking is done but also on the emotions and how they are to be addressed.

In both cases – the uncritical and anti-critical stances – any questioning of the authority for the source of an idea is avoided. The idea of 'personal authority' is given prominence. Such an attitude not only seems to challenge Christian perspectives. But ministers need to note that it is not an attack; it is already to be found in the contemporary arguments about the nature of Christian faith itself.

A mystical approach

A second area of interest is the way in which vagueness may become a virtue. New Age ideas are permeated with a sense that the world is suffused with dimensions of which we are generally unaware and that in this context obscurity is a quality. This is not the same as 'uncertainty', for the New Age proponents present themselves as certain. 'Vagueness' means the absence of boundary drawing. This is coupled with the eclecticism of stances: it is axiomatic that it is unlikely that material from any source is *a priori* to be rejected. It is, therefore, wiser to try to absorb it all rather than make selections, other than in terms of the relative importance to be assigned to data. The significance of this for Christian thinking is the rejection in principle of any idea that dogma or doctrine are appropriate vehicles for religious thought.

This assumption explains why New Age phenomena are sometimes linked with Satanism and demonstrates how something which is superficially harmless may become malign. There is a serious debate in progress about the limits of connectedness for New Age thinking and whether links with Satanism in any form are legitimate. If religious thinking is boundaryless, doctrine disappears – a state of which the religiously-minded would approve, not least because the idea of orthodox doctrine, and its correlate, 'heresy', are essentially concepts in Western religion. But one function of doctrine is not so much to keep a religion pure as to defend it against too great an intrusion (and consequently exploitation) from other sources. Thus, for instance, the Christian doctrine of God requires a doctrine of the devil or of evil, which is constructed in relation to and as part of the doctrine of God. By this means Christians keep alert to what they mean by God. Error ensues when any doctrine of the devil is separated from that of God. But when the doctrine of God itself becomes practically boundary-less and so all-inclusive, the incorporation of Satanism into Christian religion becomes possible. This shift is a mark, for example, of some churches in which vague ideas of God are sustained because highly specific beliefs in and claims about Jesus prevail. Not surprisingly in New Age activity, which is not especially Christian, such a shift may for some people become normative.

Again, it is important to be clear. Not all New Age thinking rejects Christian doctrines. It is an overview which refuses the idea that ordered reflection on belief and tradition is likely to generate and sustain faith and belief. This is especially significant for Christianity, since it raises questions about whether it is possible to articulate belief in any way. This issue is also endemic in the Church; it emerges today, for example, behind the many arguments which are sustained at different levels of church life over forms of liturgy.

Syncretism

It is inevitable that the holistic approach, with its sense of one self, one world, one earth and one universe, should also press the idea of one religion. Since much New Age thinking has developed in contradistinction to the Judaeo-Christian tradition, it has deliberately sought to absorb ideas from other religious traditions. Prominent among these have been ideas from the East, Buddhist and, to a greater extent, Hindu. In so far as New Age people are explicitly religious, they tend towards syncretism. We have already noted the importance of Teilhard de Chardin. In his theology creation is a converging evolution towards something new and higher. His understanding of Christ is similarly cosmic: he regards Christology as the evolution of the total Christ in the context of human evolution. It is not difficult to connect such ideas with the Eastern emphasis on total being and on many incarnations. These religions possess an intrinsic attractiveness, particularly in their sophisticated forms; their popular manifestations are usually not acknowledged.

An example, which permeates different levels of activity – and which interestingly has confused the Methodist Church – is the rainbow covenant. Presented as a way of committing oneself to the conservation of the world and care for the environment, this covenant involves the tying of rainbow threads (*rakshas* in Hindu usage) to the wrist. In the West this is presented as a simple act of symbolizing that the wearer is an environmentalist. But in their Hindu context these multi-coloured strings are a means of channelling psychic rays. As a result, there is uncertainty about the rainbow covenant: is it merely an attractive symbol of commitment to concern for the world? Or is it a covert way of being caught up in magical practices?

It is important, however, in considering such apparently syncretistic tendencies not to overestimate them and so treat the New Age as if it were about to become a new religion. Aspects of the phenomenon show signs of a new religious movement – an organized form of belief. But the phenomenon as a whole is unlike this. The problems for religious people, specifically Christians, occur around the fringes of faith and practice, in particular in liturgy as, for example, with creation liturgies.

These have recently been presented at St James', Piccadilly, and in a number of Anglican cathedrals. Questions have as a result been asked of bishops and other church leaders, some proponents being accused of an un-Christian syncretism. The difficulty for Christians is whether we can risk incorporating these ideas into Christian prayer or whether the Church should defend against them. The problem is not new: it perennially arises, with different responses, for example, over Freemasonry. But as with the sign of the rainbow covenant, so too with some of the liturgical language employed. Who, for instance, would be aware that a phrase like 'God's great work' has resonances of witchcraft or Satanism, unless they were listening for these beforehand? Of all the aspects of the New Age which need to be addressed by Christian churches, that of syncretism is possibly the most problematic, because it brings them face to face with their existence as *religious* institutions as well as Christian bodies.

Enlightenment, old and new

Having considered some of the phenomena which goes under the head 'New Age', the Christian is left with a sense of *déjà vu*. From a rudimentary knowledge of history we can trace the persistent undercurrent of this style of thinking and the moments when it specifically emerges. For instance, the concerns and some interpretations found in the New Age are parallel to those found in second-century gnostic thought. This was another amalgam of incompatible beliefs which held together in their social context. More recently from the early part of this century we can instance Huxley's evolutionary humanism. Mediums flourished anew in the late nineteenth century. They came more powerfully into their own because of the extensive bereavement which resulted from the First World War. In the 1960s social liberation was expressed in the Hippy movement. To some degree the residuum of this connects directly with much New Age activity.

Historians and sociologists discuss the alternative culture which lurks under public ritual observances. Working ministers who listen to those among whom they live and function are aware of this from their own experience. Beneath the veneer of formal Christianity what people actually believe is not amenable to precise examination. For example, there is said currently to be in the churches a struggle between 'conservatism' and 'liberalism'. But whenever a professed 'conservative' is scratched, extraordinarily 'liberal' beliefs may surface.

> Opinion polls do not tell us everything, but one poll taken in the wake of the 'Durham Affair' in December 1984 – commissioned ironically by the hard-line Church Society – made plain that many churchgoers remain believers despite (or because of?) their inability to swallow a lot of traditional doctrine. In the pews, large numbers doubt, or frankly do not believe, the historical status of either the virgin birth or the resurrection of Jesus, but are firm in their Christian faith and practice.[1]

The New Age phenomenon may represent the beginnings of a new religion. Inevitably adherents of existing faiths are likely to be especially blind to the nature of new religious developments. The criteria, however, for judging the potential of new religious activity are uncertain. Sociologists might see in some aspects of the New Age characteristic signs of an emergent new religious movement. Theologians might find themselves in the position of Gamaliel – unable to discount the possibility that it might constitute a development of faith. Alternatively, New Age may prove a credal *cul de sac*. And any such discussion contains the dilemma that if the New Age is given attention, it will inadvertently be assigned a social and religious significance which it does not, and perhaps should not, possess.

But that said, the Church should not first be concerned with its attitude towards the New Age. Much of the material is only of secondary interest. The challenge to and question for Christians (especially ministers) is: What, as a consequence of the issues to which New Age points, should be the distinctive emphases articulated in today's practice of the Christian faith? For example, New Age does not claim primarily to be an intellectual movement. Its primary thrust is towards the importance of feelings, whether these are recovered through lost arts, integration with nature, contact with the beyond, or new forms of therapy. By contrast, we might suggest that the formulation of Christian faith, not least in the secular world, has recently been chiefly intellectual – how and what it is possible, desirable or necessary to believe. Churches have placed a premium on contributing to the cultural and intellectual world in which they participate. This has often involved important struggles and the stance is not to be discounted. But as a result the churches' ministers may have made themselves less competent in their principal skill of providing a way of interpreting people's everyday experiences in the light of transcendence.

For example, it is becoming a point of assumed orthodoxy to argue against the so-called simplicities of dualism and to regard this as outmoded. A controversial champion of this challenge in the popular arena has been David Jenkins, the Bishop of Durham.[2] The problem, however, might be not that the academic respectability of dualistic thinking has declined. Of that there seems little doubt and much New Age reflective material argues this case. Rather, it may be that in the effort of living most people in fact think, and even experience, in dualistic fashion. Even a cardinal New Age emphasis – the uniting of opposites – has to begin with an implicit endorsement of the basic two-ness that imbues life. It is, therefore, no use telling people that they are wrong. The task is to find ways of offering an enlarging, 'gospel', interpretation of their experience.

The work of another bishop, the late John Robinson, is illuminating on this point. Intellectually he saw the weakness of the prevailing Cartesian dualism and argued against it. On the other hand, his work as a bishop among people in south London seems to have made him address religious issues repeatedly in an essentially dualistic fashion, because in experience they are inescapable.[3]

Some may regard the taking of any direction from the impact of New Age movements as a denial of distinctiveness of the Christian faith. Yet this attitude is a reaffirmation of the traditional Christian belief that growth comes about through conflictive engagement with the spirit of whatever age we happen to be in. Theological and religious ideas emerge stealthily. Old concepts are relegated and new ones take their place, usually more by a process of gentle transition than by violent replacement. For instance, in early thinking on the significance and meaning of the person of Jesus Christ, ideas based upon the Logos, the effective Word of God, as propounded, for example, in the Prologue to St John's Gospel, gradually give place to the concept of the Son. It is not that one is right and the other wrong, or that one is older and the other newer. Both are found, but during the second century the concept of Son is gradually discovered to be a better vehicle for articulating the Christian mission and understanding of God than the simpler, but more limited, idea of the Logos or Word. It may, however, be that in the late twentieth century the older notion might be revived. This option is available to the Church because it has never been lost; it has only been relegated in the hierarchy of interpretations.[4]

Other instances of such development might include the growth in theological understanding of the idea of creation in the twelfth century as a response to the emergence of Catharism.[5] Purity movements erupt from time to time.

However, the renunciation of matter by the Albigenses, coupled with their attack on the Church, made Christian thinkers face the inadequacies of their doctrine of creation and the nature of matter. The legacy of that controversy remains to this day, especially in the concept of God's creation of everything out of nothing (*creatio ex nihilo*). We might also instance the way in which doctrines of the Eucharist were clarified, but not finalized, in the controversies of the sixteenth-century Reformations throughout Europe. The need to address the challenge of science and articulate new Christian understandings has been the mark of recent Christian theology. That legacy remains as the foundations of nineteenth-century thought are themselves shaken.

There are increasing signs in the West, and not only in the churches, of post-modern fatigue. Danah Zohar describes this, using the account of the Caucus race from *Alice in Wonderland*:

'There was no "one, two, three and away", but they all began when they liked, and left off when they liked, so it was not easy to know when the race was over' . . . The Caucus-race is an apt metaphor for the post-modern, a style of thinking in which there are no winners or losers, but only unrooted conventions, all equally valid (or invalid) and all equally devoid of meaning. It is a style which has undermined sound common sense in nearly every field of contemporary culture.[6]

A similar protest is increasingly being heard from scientists, philosophers and theologians. Seminal work was done by Michael Polanyi and Alasdair MacIntyre, as well as such theologians as James Mackey, Lesslie Newbigin and Colin Gunton.[7] The psychological and social dangers of the seduction of the mind through the implicit narcissism which follows from this underlying assumption about the way to think have been exposed by Christopher Lasch.[8]

A pervasive sense of ending, which is not peculiar to the New Age, is today becoming a cultural commonplace of

Western experience. One difficulty, however, is to define which era is ending. But in general it seems a fair judgement that we feel that we are at the end of the period which has taken its direction from the Enlightenment. Peter Gay's study on the Enlightenment has been criticized, but in this passage he seems to have caught the spirit which is now increasingly generating anxiety. For 'the Enlightenment' represents not a period in history but the assumption of a distinctive attitude.

In the century of the Enlightenment, educated Europeans awoke to a new sense of life. They experienced an expansive sense of power over nature and themselves: the pitiless cycles of epidemics, famines, risky life and early death, devastating war and uneasy peace – the treadmill of human existence – seemed to be yielding at last to the application of critical intelligence . . . There seemed to be little doubt that in the struggle of man against nature the balance of power was shifting in favour of man. Men had, of course, sometimes trusted their powers before, but never so justly as now; in the eighteenth century, *for the first time in history, confidence was the companion of realism rather than a symptom of the Utopian imagination* [italics mine].[9]

The end of this confidence does not necessarily imply any return to a dark age of irrational behaviour. The chief legacy of the Enlightenment is the notion that the one way of salvation is through learning and the acquisition and ordering of knowledge. This view, however, is now giving way to a sense that there may be a series of competing offers of salvation, from which post-Enlightenment people may, because of their autonomous sophistication, choose the one which best seems to suit their particular needs. The fundamental stance common to all is that we cannot know anything for certain: we have to test what is available. In order to do that, people must abandon the constraints of any system of belief which claims that there is one way. This may be the Judaeo-Christian way or it may be the route of enlightened rationalism. It matters little. Their common error, so far as many contemporary men and women are concerned, is to claim to be the sole way to some sort of salvation.

Against this background, which provides the atmosphere in which the New Age phenomenon flourishes, we may discern three major themes which today face people and which form the context of the Church's ministry and the pastor's activity.

(a) Individual autonomy. First, there is a continuing emphasis on the problem of the autonomy of the individual. This is a 'problem' because the existential question, 'Who am I?', has been complicated by the discoveries of psychology and the other behavioural sciences. The issues cannot be compartmentalized into the realms of psychology or philosophy or religion and resolved in one of these alone.

The fact that existence has become complicated produces an instinctive distrust of any single approach to it. This is illustrated, for example, when the range of approaches to thinking about the self is listed and explored. At the beginning of the 1980s Charles Hampden-Turner attempted this in *Maps of the Mind*. This constituted 'a plea for the revision of social science, religion and philosophy to stress connectedness, coherence, relationship, organicism and wholeness, as against the fragmenting, reductive and compartmentalizing forces of the prevailing orthodoxies'.[10] He summarized and portrayed in diagrammatic form about sixty approaches to the question of human identity and autonomy, but was unable to link them to one another. The task proved impossible. The central question of existence remains as always unanswerable: now it has also become unaddressable. Consequently people live closer to the edge of primitive anxieties than hitherto.

This issue of autonomy is also connected with the disruption in previously assumed shapes for human relations, especially where power is concerned. It becomes, for example, distinctively manifest in the feminist movement.

But it is not only there. The pressure on the nuclear family and the decline of the assumption that this provides the norm for human relating for procreation and individual and social development is equally, if not more, powerful today. The Judaeo-Christian tradition is supposed to have a patriarchal pattern for such relations: the man, like God, is the head as father and source of procreative energy. However much contemporary Christian writers work to elaborate the richness and complexity within this tradition, the popular view remains that power is a simple issue in the relations of gender and within a family.

(b) We and them. The second context is the persistence of issues of peace and war. We have already discussed the obvious impact of war on this century. But war-weariness is constantly revived at an unconscious level by another pressure to fight. This results from the growth in the world's population and its consequences. Concern for the hungry and the destitute and those oppressed by war and natural disaster is continuously pressed upon people. Their generosity remains extraordinary. But the appeals are a constant reminder that the planet feels overpopulated. This generates a foreboding of permanent aggression.

This apprehension is felt in two ways. First, somehow 'we' feel ourselves to be standing, through no fault of our own, against 'them'. Guilt ensues. Second, 'they' are increasing in number and implicitly making demands upon 'us', and we are, therefore, also under threat. Both positions when studied, prove to be true and false. Each stance is regularly stirred up and people oscillate in their response.

But it is important to note that these ambivalent feelings, however we rationalize them or resolve them by good works, themselves generate feelings of aggression – ours against them, theirs against us – which produce further ambivalence. On the one hand, we know enough, indeed, too much, about war and its effects. Few, if any, anticipate war with enthusiasm. On the other hand, our defensive side is regularly mobilized, with the ensuing feeling that all life in this world is dominated by aggression.

(c) The end as universal destruction. Thirdly, the context of the Church's mission is the possibility of universal destruction. The precise means have changed, but the basic threat remains. At the beginning of the century anxiety increased with the advent of aerial bombing and chemical warfare. The end of the Second World War ushered in the era of the nuclear threat. These powerful means of extinction do not supersede each other. The crisis in the Middle East in the summer of 1990 renewed anxiety about the possibility of bombing, missile attack, chemical warfare and nuclear strikes, all at the same time.

To these are now added consternation about ecology and the possibility that the whole planet is doomed to self-destruction. While nuclear disaster required, even after Nagasaki and Hiroshima, some imagination to conceive oneself involved in it, ecological problems seem to span the chasm between the domestic and the global. The warming of the earth might produce storms which will destroy not only the ecosystem but also my small patch of garden. Of all the anxieties paradoxically that which comes closest to conception is that which is most universal.

Disorientation

These themes are not the prerogative of the New Age. The New Age material, however, regularly assigns them prominence. In so doing it indicates to the Christian Church areas of human concern which will have to be taken into account during the last decade of the millennium. The pressure for individual autonomy leads to the human potential movements. The Christian Church is reckoned to have lost its direction by getting caught between ideas of original sin and those of original value. Issues of peace and war fit the myth of the Aquarian Age, when individual peace will lead to universal brotherhood. And the prevalence of 'green' attitudes within New Age scarcely needs further mention. There is a widespread ecological concern and preoccupation with creation and nature.

When Christians first encounter an apparently alien religion, their initial reaction is usually defensive. They emphasize differences and, depending to some extent upon their theological stance, either seek to baptize the religion by pointing to the presence of Christ within it or to convert it by bringing the light of Christ to bear upon it. Few aspects of New Age activity, however, are quite so clearly alien. For they deal with areas of life with which the churches aspire to deal and they use language which either has a Christian tinge or is even explicitly Christian in content.

One way of treating such a confusing experience is to ask to what extent we can hear in it any voice of God for the contemporary Church. Denunciation is easy and usually misplaced; uncritical association is syncretistic. We need, therefore, to discover what needs to be reactivated, rediscovered or newly disclosed within our Christian tradition. This is why, as we noted at the outset, the New Age phenomenon indicates the importance to ministers of attention to the theological interpretations which reside in Christianity rather than to any new forms of action. The three major themes of New Age present themselves: therapy and the individual; spirituality in the modern context; and ecology and social responsibility. These we shall take as topics for the next three chapters. For in them we can discern a message from God to his Church.

Undergirding wisdom

The Christian tradition is both rich and flexible. This variety is sometimes treated as a weakness, but on reflection most believers have found its complications a strength to their faith. Flexibility and vitality are theologically undergirded by the idea of wisdom.

In the Old Testament the wisdom literature offers a distinctive strand of reflection about God and the world. Less concerned with locating God in history or the cult and, unlike pagan wisdom, not concerned with magic and the manipulation of power, those who believe in divine wisdom appeal to reason and experience. They express themselves in familiar categories, discerning God's teaching in everyday observations. 'You filled the earth with parables and riddles' (Ecclus. 47.15).

This leads to a beautiful set of ideas in the New Testament which interpret Christ as God's wisdom, the all-pervasive security assigned to the ambiguities and ambivalences of this world and its inhabitants. In Ephesians 3.10 this wisdom is called 'multi-faceted' or 'intricately patterned' (in the Authorized Version, 'manifold'), possibly as in an embroidered cloth or carpet. Wisdom is connected with beauty. Far from being a vague and unformed idea, it is incarnated and so becomes the cutting edge of theological tradition when dealing with the interface between divine revelation and its shadow form in human constructions.

Instead of becoming stuck with theological niceties, a wisdom-informed stance focuses upon what is commonplace among ordinary people and makes wide-ranging – and to the orthodox – risky, but still theological, connections. Among these may be some of the issues which are promoted by the New Age phenomenon. It is, then, not so much for its new insights or complexity of belief that the New Age is interesting for the churches. But the indicators of a common context which the New Age shares with the established religions are important. The churches may be blinkered because of their traditions and unable to free themselves sufficiently to discover the issues with which they need to grapple as they proclaim their gospel in the last decade of the millennium. To the three main areas we now turn.

NOTES

1 Hugh Dawes, 'Liberal Theology in the Parish', *Theology* (March 1990).

2 Much of his work has been through radio and television. But for a sense of his argument see *God, Miracle and the Church of England* (London, SCM, 1987).

3 The title of one of his last books, *Truth is Two-Eyed*, and the argument in it is one example.

4 Alasdair Heron, 'Logos, Image, Son': Some Models and Paradigms in Early Christology', in Richard McKinney, ed., *Creation, Christ and Culture* (Edinburgh, T. & T. Clarke, 1976), pp. 43ff.

5 'Catharism' describes movements throughout Christian history which call for greater purity in morals and doctrine. The Albigensian movement emerged in Albi during the eleventh century. Its members rejected the style of the contemporary Church and demanded an austere, world-renouncing life-style. The movement was finally destroyed by a mixture of military force in a Crusade and religious persecution through the Inquisition.

6 The quotation is from an article in *The Independent*. The ideas are elaborated in *The Quantum Self* (London, Bloomsbury, 1990).

7 Michael Polanyi, *Personal Knowledge* (London, Routledge & Kegan Paul, 1958), is the seminal book and often quoted by others. Alongside this we should place Alasdair MacIntyre, *After Virtue*. The works of Thomas F. Torrance have been a sustained criticism of naive dualism. Newbiggin has used Polanyi extensively in his recent book, *The Gospel in a Pluralist Society*. See, too, James Mackey, *Religious Imagination* (Edinburgh, Edinburgh UP, 1986); and Colin Gunton, *Enlightenment and Alienation* (London, Marshall Morgan & Scott, 1985).

8 Christopher Lasch, *The Culture of Narcissism* (New York, Warner Books, 1979); and *The Minimal Self: Psychic Survival in Troubled Times* (London, Picador, 1985).

9 Peter Gay, *The Enlightenment: An Interpretation. Vol. 2: The Science of Freedom* (London, Wildwood House, 1973), p. 3. Volume 1 of the set is sub-titled, significantly, *The Rise of Modern Paganism*.

10 Charles Hampden-Turner, *Maps of the Mind* (London, Mitchell Beazley, 1981), p. 8.

4 | Spirituality

It is impossible to know how subsequent generations will assess ours. But if we sought one word to mark the last quarter of the twentieth century, 'spirituality' would seem suitable. The New Age phenomenon displays great interest in spiritual attitudes and behaviour and the idea is in vogue not only among those who are publicly religious. Newspapers and magazines contain advertisements offering explorations in all kinds of spiritual quests. 'Spiritual' as an idea is difficult to define, possibly because it is necessarily imprecise. Within the Christian tradition, for example, spiritual activity ranges from the quintessentially Anglican notion that it consists primarily of going to church to ascetic and mystical practices. It is not necessary to define the concept. To attempt this would take us away from the notion of spirituality which pervades both the Church and much of our society in general. We may note, however, that we are touching an area of religious activity which is now prominent in even the most conservative traditions.

For example, traditionally Evangelical spirituality has been marked by private prayer and Bible reading during a quiet time. But in the last decade the evangelical Grove Booklet Series has included such subjects as *Developing a Sense of the Eternal* (Ian Bunting, 1985), which emphasizes the importance of imagination; *Dreams and Spirituality* (Russ Parker, 1985); *Knowing God Incarnate* (Richard Bauckham, 1983), which distinguishes such spirituality from the usual dominance of personal knowledge of Jesus. Other titles include *Praying in the Shadow of the Bomb, Indian Spirituality* (by a Hindu writer, not a Christian), *Creative Prayer*, and *Spiritual Autobiography*. We could find a similar list in almost any New Age publication: indeed some of the titles are scarcely different. Comparable literature is to be found in other branches of the Church.

Another manifestation of the spiritual quest is the way in which pilgrimage has again become important. Iona or Taizé have been to some Christians what Findhorn has been for many New Agers. They are places where a group lives a life-style that is admired and welcomes visitors. These use the experience to enable them to sustain their ideals a little longer.

For the churches there is another point worth noting. While the interest in spirituality has been confirmed by the institution – dioceses appoint spiritual directors and training is widely offered in this skill – what actually happens, what people do, occurs around the edge of mainstream religion. For example, a person may faithfully go to church on Sundays, live a Christian life at work during the week, but still seek spiritual renewal from sources which have nothing directly to do with this mainline church experience. Retreats are aptly named: they are not solely a temporary withdrawal from the rigours of daily life; they also provide an escape from the felt confines of formal religion.

The spiritual search associated with the New Age is for an alternative to ways which are already available. There is, therefore, common ground between the New Age pheno-menon and Christianity. Few would consistently claim that Christian practice is today meeting people's spiritual demands. Believers themselves find it wanting and others do not seem to expect anything from it. We should not, however, assume that because the churches seem to be failing to meet people's spiritual needs, people in general are necessarily aware of such needs. This assumption produces a marketing style of Christianity, in the belief that if the product is right, the consumers will buy it. Human behaviour is less predictable and more delicate. Ministers who are invited to handle it need to be acutely sensitive.

New Age spirituality

Nevertheless, there does seem to be a discernible despond-
ency in the sense that people have lost confidence in the
possibility of meaning. As a way into studying the possible
reasons for this malaise we can consider the style and
content of New Age spirituality. Just as the phenomenon
consists of a network of interlinking ideas, so too the
spiritualities associated with it are diffuse. This is best seen
at, for instance, the annual Festival for Mind–Body–Spirit,
at which a long menu is submitted. The 1989 Festival
offered over one hundred exhibitors, lectures, workshops
and demonstrations, child care facilities, a vegetarian
restaurant and a 'meditation sanctuary' (*sic*). Highlights of
the programme included 'How to Heal', 'The Wheel of
Karma', 'Dowsing', 'Spiritual Awakening' (by one of the
leaders of New Age thinking in Great Britain, Sir George
Trevelyan), 'Past Lives/Present Dreams', 'Psychic Development', 'Revelling in Release', 'The Carnival Within', and
'Energy Mastery'. The spiritualities, both explicit and
implicit, are derived eclectically from a variety of sources.
But while these include material from a number of religions,
it is noticeable that little is drawn from contemporary
Christianity.

The reason for this is that New Age spiritualities are
based upon the premise 'from religion to spirituality'. The
major world religions, especially the Judaeo-Christian
tradition, are believed to have failed and a new search for
knowledge, by contrast with belief, is under way:

> Spiritual or mystical experience . . . is the mirror image of
> science – a direct perception of nature's unity, the inside
> of the mysteries that science tried valiantly to know from
> the outside. This way of understanding predates science
> by thousands of years . . . A mystical experience, however
> brief, is validating for those attracted to the spiritual
> search. The mind now knows what the heart had only
> hoped for.[1]

At the heart of such a spirituality lies a longing for mystical experience which transcends those categories of existence which are today considered usual, and a powerful sense of intuition by contrast with argument. Both are undergirded by an affirmation of the irrational parts of ourselves. The resultant spirituality is expressed in a mix of nineteenth-century notions and twentieth-century psychological idiom.

The theme of spirituality most clearly exposes the American roots of the New Age phenomenon. Religion in the USA, especially during the nineteenth century, performed a different set of functions from those it played in Europe.[2] It is, for instance, often assumed that Eastern religion influenced Western mysticism as a result of the British imperial presence in India. But the connection is not so direct. During the nineteenth century in the USA belief in spiritism emerged, taking specific form in the Theosophical Society founded by Madame Blavatsky (1831–92). At that time 'science' represented the spirit of the age and theosophy claimed to complement this with its evolutionary vision in the spiritual sphere. This is not far from some contemporary reflection, not least that based upon the writings of Teilhard de Chardin. Theosophy's religious openness was not unlike that espoused by Bahai. Madame Blavatsky, partnered by Henry Olcott, went to India. The headquarters of the theosophical movement are still there. The link between the West and Eastern religion was established on a theoretical expectation that preceded actual encounter with the East. Western investment in the East, therefore, has an element of confirmation about it rather than discovery and exploration.

The pattern continued, for example, when swamis and other teachers arrived in the West during the 1960s and onwards. Prior to this esoteric forms of spirituality had been on offer, but generally to a narrow circle of adherents. It was at that time possible to think and write about each of these separately. The New Age phenomenon, however, promises to integrate this array of belief into a new synthesis. These religious movements are 'new', not in the sense of their having new content but by comparison with the old religions and social entities over against which they stand. Their newness does not consist in their referring to a phenomenon which has never appeared before. It is found in something that places itself in a new relationship to existing religious institutions, and particularly in a relationship which points to a different quality or character.

Mystical experience accompanies concern with nature and the idea of the self evolving from and through a higher evolutionary consciousness. The notion of experience on a higher plane than that on which we normally live is widespread in religion. New Age ideas about mystical experience, however, regard it as the attainable norm rather than an occasional (for some desirable) aberration. This statement, however, indicates a problem. It is difficult to reach agreed definitions of what is meant by mystical experience. One mark, however, seems to be that it consists of a temporary state, or series of temporary states, which may be sustainable for longer or shorter periods but which are not permanent. However important, therefore, mystical experience may be for a person's spiritual development – and so far as can be seen more people have such moments than are prepared to admit to them – it does not alone provide a basis on which to establish a pattern of behaviour.[3]

The spiritual quest is essentially about the integration of the various dimensions of life. Mystical experience alone is insufficient as an integrative basis. It is not for nothing that most Christian mystics have either withdrawn from the world and been admired by others or have kept their experiences to themselves as a private aspect of their spiritual lives.

New Age hopes

The mystical aspects of New Age spirituality are chiefly informed by Eastern religion and the Qabbalah rather than any Christian tradition. Whether resurgent Islam and religious struggles on the Indian subcontinent will change this attitude remains uncertain. The idealizing of Eastern religion as integrative and impressively syncretistic is a long-standing Western error and there is little evidence of its decline. However, three main emphases in this spiritual approach match aspects of contemporary Christianity.

(a) The search for experience. First there is the search for different experience. Religious people seem increasingly dissatisfied with what their own traditions supply. It is difficult to discern, however, precisely where the problem lies. It may be that the action-oriented Christianity of the late twentieth century, with its emphasis on socially responsible behaviour, has paid insufficient attention to the personal needs of the individual. The Protestant pre-disposition to identify the will of God with immersion in the world may have colluded with secularizing tendencies, which are mistakenly felt to have destroyed spiritual aspirations. Evidence suggests that they have been altered but not obliterated.[4] Any excessive emphasis on the second command-ment – to love our neighbour – is likely to put great weight on human relationships, both intimate and social, and thus encourage the idea that Christian faith is chiefly a matter of ethics.

In resisting this trend some seek a spirituality that transforms obedience to the first commandment – to love God – into separation from the world, and seek a sense of his presence through contemplation. And like much New Age spirituality, this contemplation is linked with nature and art and the sort of assumed mysticism that comes from such retreats.

It may also be that preoccupation with the individual has itself ravaged the idea of the spiritual life as engagement with the other – God – and the personal transformation which follows. The post-Freudian world is dominated by the assumption that the category of the personal is the supreme one for thinking and knowing. One Christian response may be seen in the revived interest in Ignatian spirituality and in one-to-one guided retreats. Here the

religion of personal attention receives its purest religious
rationale.

In New Age spirituality the search for the other and
concern for the self coincide in an unusual way. There is
little doubt about the emphasis upon the individual and his
or her personal enlightenment. The usual description is
'awakening'. Some people with similar interests may band
together under the banner of the New Age, but spirituality is
primarily a personal journey. Yet at the same time it is tied,
especially through its tendency to emphasize oneness with
nature, to socially responsible action, although this is often
more concerned with flora and fauna than people. Yet as
presented there is a strange sense of belonging to one another
without the need for actual association.

(b) Creation-centred spirituality. One connection between
New Age and Christian spirituality is found in 'creation-
centred spirituality'. A leading proponent of this is Matthew
Fox, a Roman Catholic priest.[5] Its public expressions emerge
in creation festivals and liturgies. For some this approach
provides a direct link between their personal needs and a
sense of that which is greater. But whereas traditionally the
latter has been a transcendent God, it now becomes a
potentially manageable nature, even if this remains an object
of awe. This stance leads to a drift towards pantheism – the
belief that God and the universe are identical. As a result
the connections with some Eastern ideas, especially those
derived from Hindu thought, become explicit.

Sophisticated Christian thinking in this field, however, is
predisposed towards panentheism – the belief that the being
of God penetrates, includes but is not coterminous with the
whole universe. There is a distinction to be drawn between
the two, but the niceties escape most ordinary believers,
who seem to lean towards pantheism. Indeed, there may
even be a Western predisposition towards pantheism, which
would also imply that Hindu thought is also congenial. The
mystical drive towards union with the divine, when freed
from any constraint of credal demand, is likely to verge on

pantheism. As always when discussing religious experience, however, the technical theological niceties matter less than their application in spiritual living.

> From my own experience, coming of age in the sixties in the midst of the moral and spiritual decadence of Western civilization as represented, for example, by the Vietnam War and from my studies at the Institut Catholique in Paris, where Thomas Merton told me to go . . . I became absolutely convinced that more Neoplatonism was the last thing the West needed. More dualisms of soul vs. body, of male vs. female, of intellect vs. creativity, of mysticism vs. politics, were the last categories to renew spirituality. It was the biblical tradition as represented by the creation theology of the Hebrew Bible, by the prophets and by Jesus, that I was looking for and that I believed many in our times were looking for.[6]

Meister Eckhart is the major historical source for this creation-centred spirituality. Most of its themes are already present in his writing – creation as blessing and the centre of Christian theology (by contrast with the fall/redemption scheme); a panentheistic stance, which might, however, be regarded as almost pantheistic; letting go and letting creation be; the divinizing of humanity; divine potential in all; Jesus as a reminder of what it means to be God's child; and laughter, newness and joy at the heart of things. All of these themes are found dispersed throughout Scripture and theological writing. It was Eckhart, however, who seems first to have distilled them into a distinctive spiritual approach.

Creation-centred reflection draws the mystical and natural together. The emphasis on intuition which is parallel to this reflection encourages the idea of removing any structure, because it is believed to be inhibiting. We have already noted how New Age generates a sense of belonging without a corresponding demand for formal association. It, therefore, has little room as yet for organization or formal leadership.

But in two major areas creation-centred thinking resonates with social issues of today.

First, although there is an increasingly optimistic attitude towards the possibility of humankind's working with rather than against nature, there is, nevertheless, no avoiding the fundamental dilemma of our relation to the rest of the world. In spite of encouragement towards an integrative style of awareness and the adoption of an anti-dualistic attitude, human beings remain obstinately dualistic: there is a 'them' (or 'it') and 'us', without which distinction 'we' should have no capacity for reflection, whether on ourselves or the creation.

However powerfully the argument is put for seeking refuge from the world or reform of it through new self-awareness, it nevertheless comes back to us as object. There remains a world outside us and from which we can differentiate ourselves. And even if we adopt a panentheistic view and try to regard God as permeating both it and us and so potentially breaking down the boundaries and barriers, we need the sense of that God as at least different, if not as 'other' as has been sometimes affirmed, if we are to have any contact with him/it – that is, if a spiritual quest is to be possible.

The second issue is the central religious question of salvation. New Age spirituality is marked by eschatological urgency, especially when linked to creation. The world faces, it is argued, a catastrophe from which we have to escape. But to do this humankind must recover a lost order to things, which is essentially an original, often pre-scientific, simplicity. The evil in the world is largely the creation of people, especially when they band together in societies. We need, therefore, a personal, social and intellectual recovery of the old simplicities. Redemption is the work of the redeemed, who will save themselves and possibly the whole world.

In this argument spirituality and human potential therapy begin to slide into one another, which is exactly what we might predict from the holistic stance of the New Age. It is also in this regard that we once again note the meaning of 'new' in the phrase 'New Age'. There is no specially new content but a new attitude and way of thinking by comparison with the collective social entities, nations, institutions, and assumptions to which New Age people are opposed. It is also at this point that New Age and New Religious Movements coincide most closely.

(c) The feminine theme. This search for the mystical and reaffirmation of intuition to some extent accounts for the feminine theme in New Age spirituality. The words 'power' and 'spiritual' are properly joined here. Creation and nature are held to be feminine concepts, because they are marked by mutuality. Such distinctiveness is regarded as feminine by contrast with the masculine proclivity to competitiveness. 'Recently a woman psychologist suggested that human survival may require the private virtues of women to go public. "Perhaps the women's movement is part of an evolutionary process that will keep us from going the way of the dinosaur and the dodo".'[7]

The overlap between feminine stances, psychology, spirituality and therapy is illustrated by the Myers–Briggs workshops. Many ministers will be familiar with this scheme of personality types, since it has been widely employed in church training programmes. They were devised by two women, Katherine Briggs and Isabel Briggs Myers, who employed Jung's theory of personality as a foundation. But the approach has many of the qualities of contemporary spirituality about it.[8] The amalgam of self-regarding examination, optimism as self-fulfilment, feminine (mutual) by contrast with masculine (competitive) assumptions, a notionally accessible divine presence in creation by contrast with ideas of God as wholly other, creates for many an attractive option.

This personal programme is then attached to a political one, with the additional suggestion, therefore, that change is not only desirable but achievable. Such intractable problems as those of arms race, economic growth and inequity, technology and its effects on the environment can be creatively and successfully addressed, so it is argued, provided that human beings retrieve those inner resources which have hitherto been ignored or denied. This recovery in particular includes specific affirmation of the feminine dimension to all thought and action. The outcome, however, is that New Age spiritual approaches become uncannily similar to those already found in the Christian tradition. There, too, the connection between individual change and spiritual direction and world change is intimate. Yet this is the spiritual tradition which is adjudged to have failed humankind.

Christian spirituality

Whatever new forms Christian practice may take in the next decade, the distinction between belonging and association may become increasingly important. The two extremes can already be discerned taking institutional form. Local churches seem to be driven to become more 'associational', while those explicitly designated by their history and function (such as, for example cathedrals) as 'communal' become more open.[9] But this polarity is not peculiar to the churches: in this field we may contrast New Age with New Religious Movements. The latter encourage powerfully binding behaviour to which their members are required to conform. New Age, by contrast, is a looser idea, consisting of associations of people who accept an overall drift of thinking but do not conform to one single practice. In this sense the phenomenon is less syncretistic than eclectic.

A similar eclecticism is a mark of the contemporary Church. People choose the extent of their association with a church rather than belong to it. The churches have not generally encouraged this stance. A statistically dominated age requires figures. Financial constraint compels planning, which means that churches need to know on whom they may or may not rely. Preoccupation with membership receives theological justification from models of the Church as 'community' and 'family'. These both meet management requirements and encourage social conformity. It is interesting to note that the new Archbishop of Canterbury and the new Bishop of London, each of whom represents a different strand of Anglican life, when asked about their plans for the future of the Church, talked about efficiency. The emotional pressures engendered by the demands of such styles of church life, however, may foster some eclectic religious behaviour in people. The demands of membership may become too great to be borne and the general feeling of spiritual need becomes divorced from church life and salvation is sought elsewhere.

If this is the case, it is likely that there will be a decline in observance of 'rules' as church members become more confident in their personal eclecticism but unwilling to desert the churches which sustain the ideals of belief and nurture it on behalf of others. Thus churches will be increasingly seen to be offering a menu from which people may select the amount that they believe and practice. This has probably been the case for a long time and the idea is difficult to test. Now, however, this attitude may become more respectable and public. Teaching about spiritual behaviour will change accordingly.

Traditionally ministers have taught their people forms of spirituality which originate from models which are to be followed. This approach derives from the concept of discipleship: the disciple follows his or her Lord as made known through the Church: worship, Scripture, tradition and teaching. As, however, people become more aware of their autonomy and responsibility (the two together being the key, not the former alone), then they feel more accountable for their own spiritual lives and seek a way that 'works'.

Ministers have two options in the face of this. Either they can try to draw the boundaries around the churches more securely and encourage conformist behaviour, which is labelled distinctively 'Christian'. Or they can try to offer a range of opportunities, within which there is no single approved way of building a spiritual life, but by using which people may be encouraged along their spiritual journey. The criterion for being Christian would then be a life-style rooted in these traditions. The present dilemma, however, is not simply a tension between these two contrasting approaches. But those to whom pastors today minister are in ultimate danger because of a lack of historical and theological awareness, which means that they are not being, and maybe cannot be, exposed to the range of options open to them. The Christian spiritual heritage offers awareness of the senses and of the mind, of feeling and of intuition, of immersion in this world and withdrawal from it, of intellectual and anti-intellectual strands.

The New Age phenomenon has something to teach the churches here. Its literature and discussions consistently call for 'metaphysical reconstruction'. This means returning behind the assumptions of the present age to those of which people have lost sight. This produces, for example, the emphasis on smallness and nature, the feminine and creation, new forms of power and social structure, and above all the holistic sense.

The matching Christian approach, something of which the churches may be beginning to recover, is a rich set of traditions which also predate the Enlightenment. The desert fathers, for instance, offer approaches for the senses (fasting), the mind (reading and reflection), the emotions (felt intimacy with God) and intuition (contemplative union). This basis was refined into the monastic spiritualities, with their differing emphases on reading and study, free-ranging emotion, an ordered structure to life through penance and engagement with the mystery, and the withdrawal through retreat and silence. The Reformation had little effect on the substance of these spiritualities, although it obviously had a political and social impact which altered their direct influence in people's lives. But these practices were not eradicated and aspects of them, especially reading and study or free-ranging emotional religion, even became more prominent. There is, then, a continuity of spirituality in the Western churches.

Many groups and centres offer tuition in these and other parts of the churches' spiritual inheritance. The reality appears to be, however, that although a range of rich opportunities can be offered and people might be encouraged to risk a greater eclecticism in their spiritual lives, this attitude does not seem to commend itself. It neither attracts the majority of practising Christians nor seems inviting to others who are looking for some spiritual directions. If ministers are to come to terms with this problem, then they need to be alert to three fundamental marks of any contemporary Christian spiritual quest.

(a) Ordered 'ad-hocracy'. Alvin Toffler has described three waves, or large-scale processes, of human development: first, the agricultural; second, the industrial, and third, the post-industrial.[10] John Robinson developed this theme and applied it to religion. He suggested that the first wave was 'epitomized within the Christian tradition by . . . "the sanctification of time" in the church's calendar and the sanctification of place in the parochial system'. The second wave, following the Reformation and Renaissance, was marked by organization into denominations and standard-ization of liturgy and Scripture. The third wave still requires clarification.

> If there is one characteristic that Toffler sees of all third wave trends it is 'demassification'. And that is as evident as it is elsewhere in all the signs of the times, morally and spiritually. There has been what Schon called a 'new ad-hocracy', in ethics and liturgy, in structure and spirituality. There is no longer a single pattern of identity in churchmanship or ministry, or even in what it means to be a Christian.[11]

The names often associated with exploration of this third wave are Thomas Merton, Teilhard de Chardin and Raymond Panikkar, all Christians who amplify their

Christian belief through links with other religious ways of thinking. Some New Age thinkers also regard them highly. It is, however, not yet possible to know whether their distinctive (almost idiosyncratic) approaches to the meaning of life and ways of living are accessible to all or to none or whether they will remain significant only to a select few. The enterprises which they attempt require not only imagination but also profound learning and intense commitment to a specific tradition. Yet like John Robinson, himself a working bishop in South London for much of his ministry, they are far from the dilettantism of some of those who have subsequently commended them.

If such wide-ranging approaches to spiritual life are to be adopted and commended, they will need paradoxically to be brought more down to earth for everyday Christians and ministers. The issue is not so much the precise content offered by these inspirers (we might say 'gurus') of the third wave as where people are to be invited to put the emphasis in their own explorations. Spiritual experience cannot be secondhand.

For this the New Age phenomenon suggests some useful directions for spiritual teachers and leaders in the Church. We have noted, for example, how it does not abandon scientific domination of the thought of this era but discounts it in favour of older, more primitive and more emotional guidance and spirituality. It also rejects the structural forms that the Christian faith has taken, sometimes with hostility. Such criticism, however, is not original: it has a long pedigree within the churches themselves and we might be inclined to ignore it. But it may indicate the core issue in spirituality to which we should attend.

As during this century the problems of articulating a sense of the transcendent have multiplied, the demand has intensified that those who profess some such belief should do so clearly. There is a sort of dependent expectation that Christians (since Christianity is the foundational religion in the West) should firmly believe what others cannot and may even be unwilling to try. There also seems to be some regret that Christians no longer struggle to believe what people wish to have kept for them as an option. The activism of the churches, while having a basis in the Christian gospel and being itself one response to an increasing sense of irrelevance, may have inadvertently obscured the foundation of that activity. This is belief in a personal transcendent being – God.

It is instructive that non-realist approaches to belief, such as recently argued by Don Cupitt, have not received widespread approbation within the Church nor become evangelistically effective. In his religious quest he has found himself, like many contemporaries, drawn towards Buddhist ideas. Yet these do not ultimately help, even if, as in Cupitt's case, preference is given to the form rather than the content and to the more philosophical pattern found in Theravada Buddhism. There may be deep social and cultural reasons why what are essentially Eastern types of belief are not universally acceptable, even in the pluralist West.

The New Age phenomenon itself tends to suggest that light is likely to come from the East and we have noted some of the forms which that assumption takes. However, such enthusiasm for Eastern styles of religious belief and expression should not obscure the considerable impact of the West upon the East, which shows no sign of diminishing. This may be a cause for regret to some people, but much of the East aspires to Western life-styles and standards of living. Even, therefore, if these were renounced by Westerners under the influence of Eastern teachers, they would be reproduced in the East. David Edwards's judgement, therefore, seems correct: 'Much of the future of the whole world will depend on what the West makes of its own religious heritage.'[12]

In a pluralist society, as each individual or group seeks its own eclectic stance by which to interpret life, the need is all the greater for some to hold to the overarching notion or concept of the transcendent. In other words, it would be impossible, or at least unlikely, that anyone could discover or articulate for themselves or with others any sense of transcendence unless in that society there were some people who unreservedly represented this and allow themselves to be so used.

One aspect of Christian spirituality, therefore, is best thought of in these terms. The churches are not in competition with other groups. Their distinctive task is by their profession of faith in a transcendent God to provide people less with a range of options than with the continued witness to the importance of that which is being pursued – the transcendent. In other words, whilst the exploration of opportunities for spiritual life is not to be decried, this takes second place in the Church's life to theological examination of the concept of God.

This understanding gives us some indication of the task of the Church in the third wave. The first, Robinson suggested, was sanctification of time and place; the second involved standardization. The third is the new 'ad-hocracy' – the eclectic style of religious life. But for this last wave to be possible, it is also necessary that some group or institution within a society sustains the concept that what is to be explored is other than the self – that is, the idea of God. The third wave, therefore, directs the Christian Church away from too great an attention to structural and doctrinal questions. These are the residue of the first two waves. Now the central spiritual task is theological – exploration of God – without which no spirituality is in the end possible. The many current concerns with the topic of 'spirituality', therefore, may be interesting to some but are ultimately secondary to the continuing life of the Church.

(b) Idolatry. Against this background, we can discern one distinctive aspect to contemporary Christian spirituality that needs to be emphasized. It arises from the interplay of public worship and private devotion in the development of spirituality. On the whole the English, and maybe all Western churches, have not managed this well. In the worlds of Toffler's first and second waves, the connection between the two scarcely needs much attention. They largely overlap.

Going to church and privately reciting prayers which have been learned by heart have comprised basic spiritual behaviour in most churches.[13] Although in the uncertainty of the third wave such connections are likely to dissolve, they should not be let go too eagerly.[14] A private spirituality which develops apart from public worship is a form of idolatry, since it encourages the creation of a personalized God, who is immune from the scrutiny of others. And public worship without private devotion becomes hypocrisy, since it can descend to being solely a series of outward observances.

Idolatry and hypocrisy are alike ultimately destructive to those who practise them. Helen Oppenheimer clarifies this point, using Peter Geach's argument on idolatry: 'In all the scriptures, he [Geach] insists, "There is not a hint that *bona fide* worship of a heathen god does the worshipper the least good": rather it alienates. It is worshipping a *nothing*.'[15]

Contemporary examples of idolatry within the Christian context, in the sense of worshipping an artefact, are few. Geach's specific objection is to inter-faith worship and its confusion with idols. But in the light of New Age approaches a modern example of being bound to an artefact might be to be constricted in our imagination and reflection to a human construction, whether material or, as more often today, mental.

This is the most serious weakness in New Age spiritual ideas; it is also a warning to the churches. We have, for example, already noted the way in which New Age thinking contributes to and endorses contemporary trends towards narcissism, which is also linked with a concern for nature. 'If the party of the ego glorifies the rational man, the party of Narcissus [i.e. human potential and New Age spirituality] seeks to dissolve tension in its own way, by dreaming of a symbiotic reunion with nature. It glorifies the natural man, often after redefining nature itself, however, as an aspect of some universal mind.'[16]

This view is uncannily like those of the prophets of the Old Testament and, in the New Testament, of St Paul's

struggles to interpret the significance of idols. The fundamental error does not lie in the act of worship, however
misguided, but in replacing that which is supernatural and
not purely a human construction with something that is
humanly conceived and created. As a result, people find
themselves in thrall to, and enthralled by, their own image.
Thus captivated, they have little chance of breaking out of
the cycle of narcissism, since every act of worship can only
confirm it.

This, as Oppenheimer also suggests, may begin to account
for the occasional connection between such worship and
Satanism. 'Some human beings easily devote themselves to
the thrills of religion, to the numinous and even the merely
spooky, letting the workaday moral claims that are bound
up in the full concept of holiness go by default.'[17] And if this
captivation is avoided, there remains enthralment to oneself
and the limitations of the world when seen only for and
through oneself. The Judaeo-Christian tradition has found
only one response to the danger that any spiritual practice
can turn malign. This is again to hold central to faith the
quest for the unknown and unknowable God rather than
any experience alone. Spiritual experience is dependent upon
theological energy and not, as sometimes suggested today,
vice versa.

(c) Renewed sacramentalism. How, then, specifically can
the Church respond not only to the spiritual questions of
today but also do this by holding to its central task of
exploring the being of God? The danger is that in perceiving
in the light of New Age and similar phenomena the
deficiencies in their belief, Christians may lose sight of their
distinctive hopes and what may be useful for others.
Worship, spirituality and even idolatry each redirect us
back to sacramentalism as the underlying strength of the
Christian stance.

Sacramental thinking holds together in earthed fashion
aspects of the range of human experience and life which
otherwise appear to be disparate. Emphasis on the

psychological side of the self in the Protestant tradition and a drift towards magic in the Catholic tradition have both tended to pervert religion. The lesser sacraments that ritualize life's transitions may be losing some of their effectiveness. Consequently new theological interpretations have been introduced. So, for instance, Christ is called the foundation sacrament or the Church is seen as the sacrament for the world. Impressive as such exercises are, they prove, however, ultimately unhelpful since they encourage the notion that genuine spiritual discernment involves our moving away from the very thing that sacraments have customarily affirmed – namely, that the presence of God is mediated to us in various ways, not least through the most ordinary and accessible materials and experiences. 'Once sacraments are understood for what they are – human creations which function as doors to the sacred – there is no intrinsic reason why new sacramental forms could not be invented to *reach the same sacred realities that the old forms once revealed* [my italics].'[18]

Sacraments viewed in this functional way unite the individual's experience with something larger – the presence of God and the shared experience of others. The Church has recently loosened contact with its theological and therefore sacramental roots. This is not a matter for the experts. By 'theology' is not meant 'doctrine', the teachings of the Church. Theology represents an attitude of exploration into God which has to be articulated. To be a theologian in this sense is part of the role of every believer and the articulation may take the form of a lived life as much as an argued piece of writing. Central, however, to such theological expression is the spiritual life of the individual and the Church alike.

For example, the churches have increasingly come to value the Eucharist as their basic form of worship, but only at the expense of diminishing, and perhaps even removing, some of its key dimensions. Twenty-five years ago Michael Ramsey commented that, while there were many benefits from this widespread recognition of the central sacramental nature of Christian worship, there had been a diminution in acknowledging the awesomeness of the memorial of Christ's death. He added: 'The responsible act of an individual . . . an act full of awe and dread . . . the awe in the individual's approach to Holy Communion, which characterized both the Tractarians and the Evangelicals of old, stands in contrast to the ease with which our congregations come tripping to the altar week by week.'[19]

Today he might have commented on the way in which a dramatic sharing of the Peace as a means of confirming the centrality of human relationships (which are justified as 'fellowship') seems to have become the focal moment in the service. It would be futile to suggest that a recovery of lost sacramental disciplines would bring to worship those who seek new spiritualities. But because the Church has lost a sense of what is awesome in its sacramental practice, we have insufficient sense of the numinous to be able to examine and explore what is being demanded of us by way of spiritual newness, both by God and by those for whom the churches still sustain some notion of God.

Conclusion

The New Age emphasis on spirituality is helpful in clarifying this dimension of the Church's life. Part of the pressure from anything spiritual that claims to be 'new' is that the Church may seek to compete or to absorb. Competition leads to judgements and to rather vacuous claims that there is nothing actually new about it, since it is already to be found somewhere in the Christian tradition. This attitude, however, takes insufficient account of the reason why people are seeking something that they believe to be new, and so avoids examination of the way that the Church is locked into its dynamic human context. That is the way of spiritual imperialism. Absorption seems to go in the opposite direction. The Church, seeing something apparently different in the spiritual world in general, seeks to make it its own. This response, especially in matters to do with so nebulous an idea as spirituality, tends to be uncritically accepting.

That way lies the danger of syncretism, rather than a positive eclecticism, and the loss of distinctiveness, which can lead to the sterility of idolatry.

Whichever stance the Church presents, however, it will not become the natural focus for everyone's spiritual aspirations. The relationships between the Church and its context now are too complex for this to occur. The New Age phenomenon is one reminder of this. With its emphasis on the importance of a spiritual dimension to human life, however, it can be illuminating for the Church. For it reminds Christians of the fundamental point of their faith: that it is about grappling with the concept of personal transcendence, the concept of God, and holding on behalf of those who cannot believe the idea of belief. There are not many plaudits for this, but in it we begin to see the nature of ministry. For this involves not only the invitation to participate in an exploration of thinking, life and spirituality which remains rooted in the richness of the specifically Christian tradition. It also includes sustaining the rumour of God, rather than any great clarity about him, thus allowing those who wish to discount it and dissociate from it to do so with some clarity and confidence.

This may not seem the most positive contribution to a Decade of Evangelism, but it could be one of the most useful tasks of the Church in the spiritual confusions and searches of the last decade of the twentieth century.

NOTES

1 Ferguson, *Aquarian Conspiracy*, p. 398.
2 W. S. Hudson, *Religion in America: An historical account of the development of American religious life* (New York, Charles Scribner's Sons, 1965).
3 Formal religious systems tend to underestimate the ubiquitous nature of such experience. Research is being continued at the Alistair Hardy centre, Oxford. See, too, S. R. Clarke, *The Mysteries of Religion. An Introduction to Philosophy through Religion* (Oxford, Blackwell, 1986); and S. Katz, *Mysticism and Philosophical Analysis* (London, Sheldon, 1978). There is a connection, too, with the thoughts of one of the gurus of the New Age, Abraham Maslow, especially *Religions,*

Values and Peak-Experiences (Columbus, Ohio, Ohio State University Press, 1964), and his posthumously-published collected papers on human potential in *The Farther Reaches of Human Nature* (Harmondsworth, Penguin, 1973).

4   The work of David Martin has been crucial in this area. There is a wide-ranging debate. For a convenient and accessible recent work see Geoffrey Ahearn and Grace Davie, *Inner City God* (London, Hodder & Stoughton, 1987), and the references there. This work is complemented by the survey reports of the Rural Church Project, especially vol. 3, *Parish Life and Rural Religion*. Outlines of the results are to be found in *Faith in the Countryside* (Worthing, Churchman, 1990), although that report seems not to use them in its recommendations.

5   His *Creation Spirituality* (New York, Bear, 1990), is the key text book, but see also his earlier *We, Wee, Whee all the Way Home* (New York, Bear, 1987). His interest in the topic was fired when he edited the works of Meister Eckhardt (see n 6).

6   M. Fox, ed., *Breakthrough: Meister Eckhardt's Creation Spirituality in New Translation* (Garden City, New York, Image Books, 1980).

7   Ferguson, *Aquarian Conspiracy*, p. 249.

8   I. B. Myers and P. Myers, *Gifts Differing* (New York, Consulting Psychologist Press, 1980).

9   The terms 'associational' and 'communal' are developed by Bruce Reed in his now well-known theory of church types. See *The Dynamics of Religion* (London, Darton, Longman & Todd, 1978). The idea has been recently elaborated in Giles Ecclestone, ed., *The Parish Church?* (Oxford, Mowbray, 1988).

10 Alvin Toffler, *The Third Wave* (London, Pan, 1981).

11 Robinson, 'Religion in the Third Wave: The Difference in Being a Christian Tomorrow', in *Where Three Ways Meet*, pp. 119ff.

12 D. L. Edwards, *Religion and Change* (London, Hodder & Stoughton, 1969), p. 234.

13 See, e.g., John Moorman, *The Anglican Spiritual Tradition* (London, DLT, 1983).

14 Robinson specifically makes this point. The 'waves' do not stand for past, and therefore finished, aspects to religious life. There is an accumulation of tradition. The spiritual danger is that we try to establish waves one or two as the norm to be recovered, rather than move on to wave three.

15 H. Oppenheimer, *The Hope of Happiness* (London, SCM, 1983), p. 149, quoting Peter Geach, *God and the Soul*.

16 Lasch, *Minimal Self*, p. 258.

17 Op. cit., p. 152.

18 Martos, *Doors*, p. 530.

19 A. M. Ramsey, *Durham Essays and Addresses* (London, SPCK, 1956), pp. 15ff.

5 | Human Potential

As it draws to a close, the twentieth century is being characterized in many ways, depending on the perspective of the person doing it. But high on the list of Western preoccupations is the prominence of therapy and attitudes which originate from it.* We need to ask ourselves what this dominance is and why it is occurring now.

Within the New Age the human potential approach is especially prominent. The phrase 'human potential' itself sounds different from 'therapy'. The latter implies the need for healing; the former suggests undiscovered strengths through recognition of which people might improve themselves and the society within which they live. The distinction is valid, although both human potential and therapy are based on the philosophical foundation of individual autonomy. Most therapies are oriented towards the past. They seek to clarify a person's history in order that he or she may live more competently in the future. Potential, by contrast, carries implications from the discovery of present strength which can change the future. Most therapy also tends to be analytic; human potential is more synthetic and eclectic. It brings together a range of stances with little regard for consistency of theoretical foundation. This may be because the basic concern is survival and coping.[1]

---

*The term 'therapy' is itself culturally conditioned. In the USA, for instance, it is widely used to describe relations between a patient and analyst or client and counsellor, without the implication that a mental illness is being treated. It is more akin to the notion of an inadequacy being relieved or a wound healed or even a confusion clarified. By contrast, to be 'in therapy' in Great Britain conveys a stronger sense of weakness or sickness, unless the phrase is being used in among the small coterie of analysts and therapists. In this chapter the more general sense is employed.

The human potential approach separates therapy from sickness. It takes a range of psycho-technologies and allies them to a firm belief in individual autonomy.

The paradigm of the Aquarian Conspiracy sees human-kind embedded in nature. It promotes the autonomous individual in a decentralized society. It sees us as stewards of our resources, inner and outer. It says that we are *not* victims, not pawns, not limited by conditions or conditioning. Heirs to evolutionary riches, we are capable of imagination, invention, and experiences we have only glimpsed. Human nature . . . has only to discover itself.[2]

The prevalence of therapy

Contemporary interest in therapy is not a response to increased sickness. It is an aspect of a larger phenomenon: the influence of the assumption of the autonomy of each individual. Self-help and responsibility are emphasized in most modern therapies. But it is increasingly becoming clear that this ideal of autonomy produces a fundamental ambiguity. When this is affirmed, it seems to open up new possibilities of life, both for the individual, whose authority is confirmed, and for any community of such autonomous individuals. But when this ideal is lived in practice, it seems to lead to its own destruction. For example, we may suggest that one task of the family is to encourage and enable the growth of its members, especially the children. It is important that their autonomy be acknowledged. Yet when individuals claim this, they seem to become agents of destruction of the family unit. To avoid this they seem to have to accept some diminution of the self in order to allow the family as a whole to survive.[3]

There are, therefore, unresolved philosophical – we might say spiritual – problems, as well as practical ones, with contemporary assumptions about autonomy. As a result, the more pressure these bring to bear on people and their way of life, the more individuals feel that they are being required to carry greater obligations than they bargained for.

Such stress induces in people that need for another person in their own image which is a mark of the therapeutic search. People seek a relationship to complement the self, but which does not diminish their sense of their own autonomy. The therapeutic liaison effectively meets this need: the other (the therapist) will take whatever form I may wish or need, but will do so on my terms, since I pay the fee. Whatever, therefore, is surrendered to create the new relationship, my sense of control, the autonomy which forms the philosophical or religious basis of my world view, is not compromised.

There are three key points to note about the pervasiveness of therapy. First, the relationship between patient and therapist assigns value: 'I' am listened to. Consequently therapy may enable me better to value myself and maybe others. But underlying this is a further crucial valuation: I pay for the privilege. As well as being listened to, the patient can believe that he or she is also heard. A world which feels dominated by more speakers and fewer listeners creates an urgent desire in many people to achieve such hearing, whatever the cost in effort or money.

Secondly, in therapy the patient or client finds legitimate space in an overfull life. The demands on people, especially those who are successful, are such that they are scarcely allowed to acknowledge gaps or unused space in their lives. Leisure has been taken over for business purposes: meals, sporting events, and, most popularly, the golf course. But since all these spaces have been seized, stressed people may need to find other spots for themselves, which, however, they have to justify as other than leisure. Therapy meets this requirement perfectly: the demands of life make it essential; yet it is inviolable space, for which a fee is charged – i.e. it has an assignable value within the prevailing culture.

Thirdly, the therapeutic process confirms that during the most profound exploration (even dissection) of ourselves, we each remain autonomously a reference for ourselves. The pressures which have brought someone into therapy may have indicated that a person possesses limited scope and capacity. Nevertheless, because he has found in the therapist a legitimate 'other', his own individuality is confirmed. The underlying assumptions of the spirit of the age, to which he seeks to conform, are not severely challenged.

In an unconsidered rush towards counselling models, the Church may underestimate the different ways in which the gospel addresses the same human concerns. For instance, being valued (listened to) is traditionally a central theme of confession. The decline in the practice of sacramental confession in the Catholic tradition may be a mark of the churches' failure to perceive this aspect to it. The Protestant tradition replaced sacramental confession with the offer of spiritual counsel. But because people now regard both as means of control, they no longer expect to be heard. Yet a mark of contemporary churches, whatever their convention, is the way in which spiritual direction and counsel are being rediscovered as a function not solely for the clergy but for Christians among themselves.

The second theme, provision of legitimate space, is one way of looking at public worship. The hour or so on Sunday is functionally (though in few other ways) analogous to the hour of therapy. It consists of legitimate space, since attendance has become an expression of individual preference which for many retains its social propriety. Church buildings also provide a numinous space.

Thirdly, the sense of the other is specific in religious activity, since that other is God. The question of how legitimate is an 'other' or transcendent God, is therefore once again an imperative issue for Christians. The trend to therapy is a conspicuous search for that other with whom I can be in relationship. Human potential locates it in some part of myself, where hitherto hidden resources reside. But the same thrust is apparent in therapy in general – the search for relationships with otherness. This other, called 'God', may be 'our God' or the revealed God of revelation. But whatever the object, the dynamic of the search is the same as that in therapy. Hence, when the followers of New Age advocate human potential, Christians should see them less as anti-Christian than as indicating to the churches a continuing human search.

The basis of a Christian response

A Christian response in this context cannot consist merely of a proclamation of an alternative. Such behaviour looks like the last defensive claim of an institution that has lost whatever power it once possessed. Churches – and ministers in particular – have to take account of the changed environment in which they are working. But in order to do so they need a more profound awareness of what they may stand for in the swirl of anxiety at the end of the century. They should not, therefore, begin with questions of God but at a more functional level.

Today's dilemma for the individual may be seen as something like this. Each person knows that they are not completely and solely responsible for who or what they are. The boundaries which define the individual have been enlarged. We have shifted in our perception from being creatures who were substantially at the mercy of fate. Most people now assume (whatever their creed) that we exercise some control. Consequently, the format of existential *Angst* also changes. It is no longer a randomly directed rage against a world which we inhabit or create. It becomes more focused within human relationships, which may be at the intimate level of one-to-one or even on the scale of international relations. Any expression, therefore, of self-awareness tends to seem aggressive.

Pugnacity is usually expressed in terms of space and boundaries: you shall not trespass on my territory by interfering in my life. Thus as our awareness of our own boundaries has enlarged, so the felt need to defend them has become more acute. People claim greater independence for themselves. In the process, however, other boundaries are obscured. So, for example, interest groups form. These consist of people who feel that they have sufficiently coterminous boundaries in one or two areas of their lives to define themselves enough to be able to stand together in opposition to others.

This dynamic produces the sectarian tendency which seems to mark a pluralist society. Self-selecting groups form around issues or ideas or even more primitive feelings, such as are aroused by sex or race. The regulation of life between them becomes increasingly a function of the legal system, which, because of the absence of agreed shared values, is itself perceived as yet another such interest group. The churches also participate. Within them today interest groups multiply and the process is legitimated through ecumenism. In the ecumenical movement churches move towards sufficiently identical beliefs and practices to appear to be liaising. Local manifestations of the same activity may be seen in the growth of sectarian churches of like-minded believers. The United States is the best demonstration. Within that pluralist society churches proliferate in a way as yet undreamed of in Great Britain.

The individual awareness which produces such associations also makes the experience of relationships between people and institutions fragile. Paradoxically, therefore, the emphasis on autonomy generates a spiralling sense of personal insignificance. As the boundary of the self is defined more precisely, it feels more restricted. Relationships become more fraught and have less capacity to sustain divergence. Their threshold for breakdown is lowered. There is little point in preaching or inveighing against this. It is a mark of the pluralist world which Christians need to grasp and interpret before they respond.

In order to interpret, however, we need a concept with which to work. The word 'boundary' has already been used. The line occurs in a popular song: 'You've got to have skin, to keep the outside out and the inside in.' This is a memorable, if inelegant, description of the function of boundaries. They may be turned into defensive barriers, in order to protect the self from others. But a boundary is not necessarily a barrier: it is always in principle permeable and thus simultaneously performs a number of functions. Personal boundaries, for instance, make both self-definition and relationship possible. They contain many of the pressures of everyday life as they are experienced and shared, in such a way that they are not destructively unleashed.

In any Christian response to the issues which lie behind human potential and what it may signify, we need a clear concept of what such boundaries may be. Individuals live in relation to others and in relation to their own past and future. So, for instance, there is a boundary between, say, childhood and adolescence. It is not precisely drawn and is an area of controversy between parents and children. But everyone involved is aware of it. More obvious are those boundaries which are given public significance, such as those between a single and paired state – marriage or a similar commitment – or between work and retirement. Life can be regarded as a series of transitions over boundaries, each of which involves the sadness of the loss of past security and the excitement (or anxiety) of the gain which comes from a new risk.

In this way of looking at things religion is concerned with ultimate boundaries. As we progress through life, we become at each transition more aware both of our selves, of our vulnerability, and of our mortality. What we have been and are becoming strikes us, often when we suddenly discover in ourselves behaviour that we had despised in our elders and sworn never to emulate. And at the same time the demands of a new phase of life become too obvious for comfort. A transition may thus also act as a moment of disclosure of ultimate boundaries to life. Solutions have to be sought to the questions whence I came and why and whither I am going and why. These questions address the core of my autonomous self; but they can only be asked because of my experience with others. I am thus drawn out of myself into relationships with others in order to deal with issues which may feel private and only to do with myself.

For example, the issue of my own origins arises when I confront birth. But I cannot face my own birth: that is an inaccessible event. I only consciously encounter it through someone else's birth.* We also face our mortality chiefly through the death of others. There is, therefore, a significant dilemma for many people. On the one hand, the therapeutic impact is to heightened awareness of the self. This leads to a stronger sense of boundaries and transitions across them, especially as relationships change. On the other hand, a sense of any transition increases awareness of the ultimate boundaries. These in turn bring together life and meaning, at a time when the primary source of meaning – religion – is widely discounted. Many people, therefore, have insufficient context in which to attempt interpretation of these aspects of themselves, from which their heightened sense of autonomy derives. This is the psychological background to human potential and the therapeutic dimension of the phenomenon of the New Age.

Three practical consequences ensue for today's churches. Each is a preoccupation of the contemporary Church but they are not being considered in this specific context: (1) an anti-sectarian stance; (2) the recovery of sacramental thinking; and (3) more direct attention to worship.

An anti-sectarian stance

Debates about the Church, its nature, task and future strategy abound. Some are sociologically informed; others begin from a notionally independent theological standpoint; some try and work with as much evidence from as many sources as the authors can handle. To some it seems that churches are increasingly opting, for whatever reason, for what is generally (though not technically) called 'sectarian' behaviour. Questions of orthodoxy and the content of belief

---

*It may be that it is possible to provoke a birth experience through drugs or some other means. But in spite of any claims made, it cannot be known that the experience induced is of *my* birth.

are given renewed prominence and the trend is towards conservatism of various kinds.

Fashionable forms of church government work in ways which confirm this sense. Synods, conferences, boards and councils vie to speak with authority for 'the Church', as if this were one group with a separate existence alongside other groups in society. It is dangerous to extrapolate from political changes, which may prove more temporary after the event than at the time. But over the past ten years the Church of England, for instance, seems to have been increasingly treated by politicians and the mass media as an identifiable entity rather than an influence. This attitude may also have encouraged a heightened sense of self-awareness in the Church. Finding itself used in this fashion, it becomes more anxious that it should be accurately perceived. Preoccupation with its own boundaries ensues, whether social (membership) or theological (orthodoxy). If the appointment of a new archbishop in any way reflects the state of the Church, then George Carey's first pronouncements have not unexpectedly been about both of these topics.

One prominent response which has gained widespread support at every level of church life has been an emphasis on 'community'. This ill-defined term is used to encourage a sense of joining a fellowship or association. For example, churches of all denominations organize themselves into small groups for study, prayer or charismatic praise, so that members may feel that they belong. These nostrums are a form of therapy, offering to the like-minded a sense of intimate relationship rather than of awe at the eternal dimension to existence.

This familiar side to church life may seem to have little connection with therapy and in particular human potential. Yet both represent responses to the felt, but not usually articulated, problem of autonomy in the individual and its social consequence. Both lead to incipient narcissism. The myth of Narcissus is not about self-love: it is a story of what happens when we confuse the nature and function of boundaries. 'Narcissus drowns in his own reflection, never understanding that it is a reflection. He mistakes his own image for someone else and seeks to embrace it without regard for his own safety.'[4] The narcissism of human potential lies in the blurring of me and not-me into one, so that the individual believes himself or herself to be in principle self-sufficient. The sectarian style of church life embraces a reflection of itself and is deluded into believing that it is thereby creating the Kingdom of God. An approximation of the Church to the Kingdom follows at the level of feelings, whatever the intellectual affirmation of their distinctive existence and relationship. Such behaviour in each case avoids examining boundaries and so becoming seriously engaged with others, and cocoons the world into one of the individual's or church's own devising. On such a basis it is unlikely that the Church will be looked to for anything.

In the light of this understanding, however, the churches might perceive the importance of their deliberately trying to sustain an anti-sectarian stance. They would then discover that important dimensions to their life and that of others emerge, which at least include the following ingredients.

The first discovery would be of a renewed willingness to risk the Church's belief in the interests of people's minimal, and probably confused, groping after some sense that there are ultimate boundaries and that they are managed by someone or some body – perhaps priest or church. At the basic level of everyday ministry this means spending time and effort on such simple contacts as those created by baptisms, weddings and funerals and other occasional encounters. It also requires the development of a theology to undergird this ministry, not one that is assumed to prescribe whether such ministry is performed at all. In a book which I wrote on this topic in 1985, the Preface included the following: 'One person on reading a draft commented that it made the job of the minister seem very demanding, very responsible and very important. It is.'[5]

Since then I have noticed that churches in which these

encounters are seen as opportunity rather than problem generate meeting with many other people. This is an instance of the practical difference between a sectarian and an anti-sectarian attitude. This does not lie in whether or not the occasional offices are performed for those who ask for them. Rejection or acceptance of these people is often taken to be the touchstone. But this is not so. To respond here is taken by others than those involved as a sign of a church which is confident enough in its boundaries to use them as points of engagement with them. The offices themselves symbolize the nature of the Church and are not just the concern of those asking for this ministry.

Obviously no one could claim that these are the sole point of a church's hope of interpreting life. But while there is still some evidence of a decline in the numbers of those seeking such contact, it is by no means proportional to the numbers attending church.[6] There remains evidence for an expectation that the Church will continue to embrace an anti-sectarian culture. If ministers can grasp the fundamental nature of what they are being invited to handle, a less pragmatic response may ensue.

Behaviour associated with New Age is frequently ritual-istic – a reminder to the churches of the importance of ceremonial in people's lives, especially at transitions. There may be some collusion between those brought up in the era of confidence in secularism and the churches to sustain the myth of progressive secularization and consequent irreligion. Such an attitude generates parallel certitudes: the one that religion and God do not matter; the other that they matter so much that they need to be protected from corruption. The resurgence of ritual in New Age activity reminds us that people still seek to align their lives with another felt power. In New Age this is likely to be nature or a similar source of energy. People's capacity to seek and find ritual expression of their belief, whatever form this takes, seems inexhaustible. Churches which become fearful of their being used for this purpose are likely to find themselves passed by and ministers who fail to act in such fashion will be rightly ignored.

One of the most interesting aspects of my work with clergy and churches over the past few years, however, has been the way in which more seem to be quietly recovering confidence in a vocation to *religious* activity with and for people. Consideration of the background to the New Age phenomenon specifically stimulates Christian churches to such reflection and action. Churches, especially their leaders, also have to become more confident in religion as such and less defensive of Christianity as a religion. But that is uncomfortable, because of the intimate connection between religion and irrationality.[7]

The recovery of sacramentalism

Secondly, we may notice the need to recover sacramental thinking. We have already discussed one dimension of this under the heading of 'spirituality'. That it should recur here, however, is not surprising. For one mark of contemporary therapy, especially human potential, is the way in which it increasingly seems to shade into what is otherwise known as spirituality. This drift is also intriguingly a problem both for secular therapists, who are sometimes surprised to find themselves dealing with more than therapeutic matters, and for ministers of religion, who are unsure where spiritual counsel ends and therapy begins.

Any talk of 'recovery' seems to imply conservatism or a return to a lost, but longed for, past. After an era during which almost all the churches have returned the Eucharist to the centre of their worshipping life, it may seem perverse to suggest that they need to recover sacramental thinking. We are not, however, here considering the Church and the theology of sacraments, but an attitude or stance towards the world.

During the second half of this century the various Christian churches have become more conscious of their distinctiveness and the riches that they each hold in trust. This awareness has both resulted from and contributed to ecumenical endeavour. And, as at other moments in history, the sacraments (specifically the Eucharist) have become a focus for discussing both differences and similarities between churches. One outcome, however, has been (perhaps unwittingly) a drift into a predominant assumption that they are significant only for churches and believers. They have been regarded as specifically Christian and their function as natural symbols, although noted, has not been assigned great pastoral or theological prominence.

Sacraments, however, are points where religion in general and Christian interpretation intersect. They are, therefore, too important as an interpretative medium to be surrendered solely to inter-church discussion and intra-church activity. They give a distinctive style to worship, which 'does not claim to be anything else than the quintessence of human life'.[8] Both Catholic and Reformed traditions have affirmed the evangelical thrust of sacraments. 'If the Christian faith is to maintain its identity, the only legitimate liturgical revision of the *aggiornamento* kind would be one which, perhaps by a renewal of images and concepts, reasserts the meaning and values [i.e. the transcendent meaning and values revealed in Jesus Christ] in all their ultimacy and universality.'[9]

The decade which will take the world to the end of this century is, according to New Age thinking, crucially transformative. Ecological disaster may strike; astrological prediction abounds; and new means of controlling powers which lie beyond us need to be devised. The Church's advertised project, The Decade of Evangelism, is more culturally conditioned than may be recognized. Like the New Age approaches it is preoccupied with power and how to harness it. Some speak of releasing the power of the Spirit. Others of the power of the gospel being brought to bear on the human condition. Some believe that success will follow the appointment of powerful people as special evangelists.

Frenetic activity of this sort is rarely justified. To be

saved from such folly in this decade the churches need to pay more attention to the context to which the New Age phenomenon alerts them. For example, we may be moving into an era when symbols, with their richness and variety, may again become usable vehicles for interpretation. Clarity of verbal expression will probably not be given such status as hitherto. The visual media may particularly contribute to this trend, as we have noted in the discussion of spirituality.

But there is another factor: the contrast is not between symbols and words but between styles of offering people opportunities for discovering meaning. If belief in individual autonomy is proving constricting, then one way of enlarging individuals' boundaries is not to urge them into closer association with others – the approach which draws people into community – but to expose them to the range of other dimensions to the world of which they are unaware or of which they have lost sight.

This language is characteristic of human potential, with its implicit suggestion that we can and should recover something which has been lost and the hint of hidden depths or recoverable mysteries. There is, however, an important difference. One attraction of much New Age material is its confidence in notions of hierarchy. Some, for example, possess the knowledge and may release it to their disciples. Or there is a progression of stages of awareness through which the initiate may ascend. Some find it attractive that seriousness in religion may require an arduous progression through acquired learning and experience. Here religion and therapy connect, since both are suspicious of instantaneous cure or conversion. It is instructive to observe the way in which churches which emphasize conversion experiences, for instance, also most eagerly consolidate them through rigorous follow-up teaching or personal tuition. The therapeutic disclosure is always to be tested by further examination. There is a feeling that what is instant is necessarily shallow or unimportant. Here the sacramentalism of the gospel comes in as a corrective, since such belief is false on two counts.

First, it contradicts the model of Jesus Christ. The stories of his ministry emphasize his willingness to trust the moment. This is the distinctive mark of his parables, sayings and miracles. Each is for the moment and becomes a problem when extracted from that instant. There is little or no cumulative teaching or suggestion that there should be a progression of learning. The discourses in St John's Gospel may seem to contradict this picture. But on closer examination they prove to be repetitive around nuggets of teaching rather than a progressive argument.[10]

Second, it loses contact with the sacramental nature of the gospel. Sacraments are instantaneous and multi-faceted. They can only be experienced here-and-now and, although they are shared by many, their impact on any one participant is unknown. Sacraments provide opportunity for momentary encounter with God, which is all that humankind might be able to stand. In the Eucharist a piece of bread and a sip of wine focus eternity. They thus become paradigms by which we may discern that same eternity in other moments of life. In baptism water performs the same function.

But in any sacramental act there has to be a specific moment when the large natural symbols are risked – water is poured, bread is broken and eaten and wine is drunk. These instants are opportunities for misunderstanding and misuse, which are so great that the Church has frequently tried to ensure that what 'ought' to happen actually occurs. The ideas of progression and of a hierarchy of learning, which mark the New Age material, exist in the Christian tradition because of this defensiveness. Who may preside? Who may participate? What qualifications are required? – these are the sort of question that dominates debate over sacraments. But when these topics are seen in a wider context, they emerge not as questions about God's relationship with his world but as examples of religious structure. A reminder from the New Age of this context, therefore, summons the churches back to a lost dimension of their sacramental theology and practice – the intrinsic risk and prodigality of grace with which God acts.

Whatever the long term effect of participation in a

sacramental act, in experience it crystallizes a series of instants into one moment. For that instant the participants are put in touch with something beyond themselves. The transitory nature and profound richness of sacraments as transformed and transforming natural symbols is something to which consideration of the New Age pushes Christians. An anti-sectarian stance coupled with a larger sacramental theology are keys to evangelism in this decade.

The significance of worship

These two points coincide in the third issue to which the human potential and other therapies direct the churches – a renewed consideration of the fact of worship. At first sight, when liturgical study and the resultant outpourings dominate a church's life to an unprecedented degree, this may sound a tired proposal. But in what follows our concern is worship, not liturgy.

Worship is indisputably a primary activity of the Church. It has been for most Christians a regular and frequent practice. Its customs range from the daily monastic offices through to the emphasis on the Sunday meeting. But behind both approaches lies the same principle: God is to be worshipped on the basis of a regular commitment. Underlying this demand lie other assumptions about the way that heaven and earth are linked and how the individual may approach God. There is, however, a second aspect to worship, by which events or occasions are sanctified. These episodes are not regular: they happen as and when life demands it. The Book of Common Prayer encapsulates this range with its emphasis on the regularity of the daily office, Morning and Evening Prayer; an invitation to frequent communion; and its provision of prayers and services for occasions – drought, war, sickness and so on. These special occasions in particular occur when a sense of power and control needs confirming or asserting. One area of life in which worship becomes prominent, therefore, also concerns human potential – the need for power.

We have noted that today individuals are increasingly seeking legitimate space in their lives and that therapy offers this. The churches have overlooked, especially because of their preoccupations with liturgy instead of the function of worship, that in public worship – the word 'public' is important – they offer something similar. An act of worship provides an environment which is temporary, spacious and legitimate.

Obviously this is not the sum of what worship is about. But it is a dimension of which we are reminded by the contemporary prevalence of therapy. Liturgical correctness is not the issue; a different model of worship is required. For example, it is not necessarily regular. The idea that the Church might build up people with a rich store of religious and worshipping experience may be in terminal decline. Not only has a generation passed with less knowledge of the Christian tradition and its language; the next generation may not even wish to learn this in order to participate. If, however, occasions for worship are conceived as moments when space is offered to people for their associations, then the emphasis will fall on the process of worship at least as much as on its content. The shape of the liturgy will become as much the transmitter of the message as the content.

From time to time individuals may need to regress in order that they may resume competent living.* Reed elaborated the concept of 'regression in the service of the ego' in thinking about worship of which the churches need to take greater account. In passing it is interesting that he explicitly compares the conditions for worship with those for therapy.

> Creative regression to dependence requires a suitable setting, what Winnicott calls a 'facilitating environment'. In psychotherapy this is provided by the physical setting, and by the attention, understanding and security conveyed

---

* 'Regression' in this context carries no pejorative overtones. The word describes the process of return to an earlier developmental or emotional state.

by the therapist. In worship also it is conveyed by the surroundings and by the quality of attention conveyed by those who lead it. In these and other situations, however, creative regression is only possible if the individual, or group of individuals, is able to use the conditions provided.[11]

This approach indicates a point which the churches are in danger of overlooking, namely that the process of the activity of worship is *theologically* integral with the content. Discussions today are usually about the connection between contemporary worship and moments in the historical tradition of the Church. They may also involve scrutiny of the theology implied by the content of prayers, hymns, Scripture and preaching, as well as the arguments about the sacraments. Yet worship is a human activity and consideration of it must also include an examination of what it may signify for the participants. If we see this as facilitating regression in this positive sense, the churches will be able from their rich store to offer opportunities for worship of which people may take advantage.

Thinking like this, for example, directs attention to practical questions of pace and style in the context of the process through which people are being carried. For such a task the Alternative Service Book is proving inadequate. Church discussion has tended to centre on its historical justification and the richness or banality of the language. But this is not the primary concern: it is whether the services provide the space for creativity that is required not only by the regular worshipper but even more so by the casual seeker. Liturgiologists seem to have recognized a weakness here, since they are producing more alternative liturgies for special occasions. Although the content of these is still dominated by a view of the Church as an association of people, the fact that they are published at all may suggest a growing awareness of the problem.

Ministers often testify that people comment some time after a service that they cannot remember the detail but they have been and are affected by what happened. Human potential not only suggests to the Church that its theological objection to such self-reliance needs better articulation; it also reminds them that their central activity for remaining in touch with that which transcends – the worship of God – cannot become so esoteric that the human dimension of regression is discounted.[12]

A profound difference

The prevalence of therapy, and in particular human potential, draws the Church's attention to some issues to do with human life and to aspects of the Church's resources which are in danger of being overlooked. But in spite of these similarities and the stimulus they afford, there remains a central difference between human potential and Christian attitudes.

Human potential conceives power as something that ultimately resides in the individual. In order to mobilize this potency he or she needs some form of enlightening or, as it is usually called, 'awakening'. This occurs through a transformative experience, which may originate anywhere. Marilyn Ferguson, for example, lists nineteen areas of learning which are known to have acted as triggers. They range from study courses and quasi-religious activities to sport and retreats. 'All of these approaches might be called *psychotechnologies* – systems for a deliberate change in consciousness. Individuals may independently discover a new way of paying attention and may learn to induce states by methods of their own devising. Anything can work.'[13]

The New Age literature offers such opportunities in abundance. They have in common the idea of integrating the self in such a way that hitherto undiscovered resource is made conscious. Human potential thus shades into spirituality. But two points of reflection belong here, since they concern therapy. The first is the notion of integration as healing or wholeness; the second is the question of where power for change is to be found. Both issues are also central to Christian faith. Healing is traditionally to do with the question of forgiveness and reconciliation; the source of power opens up belief in a transcendent God.

Human potential, as the phrase suggests, ideologically takes an optimistic view of human nature. By contrast Christian teaching seems pessimistic. It speaks of a fallen or depraved human nature, which tends towards sin and is always in need of forgiveness. There is, therefore, an irreducible conflict between these two understandings of human nature. But if the churches are to offer the distinctiveness of the gospel in a therapeutically dominated world, they need to understand the ground of this difference. This lies less in alternative estimates of human capacity than in disagreement over the second point: the issue of God. Again, therefore, we note the intimate connection between the questions posed by New Age spirituality as well as by human potential therapy and the similar ground on which the Church has to respond to both. Broadly speaking, within the field of human potential the basic belief is that the self is isolable, while the Christian message is that it cannot be separated from the question of God. This leads to a further distinction between these two attitudes, which resides in what we do with transcendence. Do we think of 'the transcendent' or of a transcendent *God*?

Much New Age material accentuates the importance of the transcendent but on the whole depersonalizes it. It may, for example, refer to 'divinity' in general or employ a composite phrase, such as 'God/Goddess/All that Is'. Problems of how to describe and refer to God are not peculiar to this material. They have been, and are, also the subject of much Christian writing. But in the latter the intimate connection between theology and practice or between the theoretical articulation of belief and its expression in worship provides explorable alternatives for addressing God. The New Age material lacks such opportunity, largely because it is actually addressing the self under the guise of confronting that which is other.

One way in which human potential deals with problems

of meaning is to remove distinctions. For example, selfhood is treated as an outmoded concept, since it is the rational ego which has brought about so much disaster and which limits people's potential. This stance sets up a polarity between what it calls the Western cultural tradition, which takes the rational ego as the ground of individualism, and a New Age rejection of this in favour of a new perception of the self.

The legacy of the Judaeo-Christian tradition may be found in both understandings. But that tradition itself stands for a stance on the individual which differs from both. The person is perceived as existing in a series of interlocking relationships – between the self and God, the self and one's neighbour and the self and oneself.[14] Therefore, individual identity is inseparably connected in some way (that phrase covers most points of dispute) with the existence and nature of God. The emphasis is on exploring the category of the personal.

It can be argued that depersonalized concepts of divinity will not suffice when we direct attention to people's experience, since their attractions eventually prove deficient because the connection between them and human experience is insufficiently strong. In his steady quest away from conventional theism, for example, Don Cupitt has rightly moved through and beyond notions of 'the transcendent' or 'the divine'. 'We have to cleanse ourselves of the old will to downgrade the manifest by looking beyond it to something else that is ranked higher than it . . . Hidden entities of every sort are ghosts hungry for blood, who want to suck the value out of life.'[15]

By contrast with the rigour of this argument, however, the generalized conception of 'the divine' which marks much New Age writing becomes stuck in unclarity. Such vagueness is unlikely to sustain people for long, since it ignores the complementary need for the rational to mesh in some way with the irrational. Thus an affirmation of the transcendent God will remain necessary, if people are to find space for personal reorientation and social living. The emergence of the human potential movement may distract churches from thinking about their interpretation of human life and encourage the shift towards therapy. But the critical question for the churches in the decade is in fact that of how God is to be perceived.

One reason why vagueness will prove unsatisfactory is that it encourages attractive notions of harmony which, however, take insufficient account of the experienced realities of human behaviour. There is today a widespread assumption, which is integral to human potential and underlies many therapeutic approaches, that nature, which includes human nature, is intrinsically good. It is, therefore, desirable, both for the welfare of the individual and the good of society, that we recover natural harmonies that have been lost. But the idea of the essential goodness of nature requires something other than optimism to sustain it. Historically that belief has been preserved by the understanding of nature as creation, something which is objective and therefore in principle intelligible. Human beings could investigate it because, being made in the image of God and therefore rational creatures, they were involved in, but differentiated, from nature.

This belief, however, is challenged by New Age thinking, which tends to dissolve differences or dualities, whether between human beings and the natural world or between the natural world, including mankind, and God. But once these are surrendered little space is left for interchange to occur and the positive aspects to human existence, which the Judaeo-Christian tradition has affirmed, decline. For without differentiation, there is no space between individuals and their environment, whatever that may be – the world, relations, neighbours, or God. In Christian theology, without such space there is no operating area for the Holy Spirit, and therefore no creativity, imagination and life.[16]

If men were moved solely by impulse and self-interest, they would be content, like other animals, simply to survive. Nature knows no will-to-power, only a will-to-live

. . . Even those who understand the 'wide gulf between the purely natural impulse of survival and the distinctively human and spiritual impulse of pride and power', as Reinhold Niebuhr once observed, too often tend to seek a quick and easy return to the harmony of a purely natural existence . . . Such a program [sc. to regain the innocence of nature] misunderstands human freedom, which makes it impossible to recreate natural harmony in history. The innocence of nature is harmony without freedom.[17]

The reference to Niebuhr in this quotation is significant. For he discerned the essential correlation between differentiation (a powerful sense of sin), human freedom and belief in the reality of a transcendent God.

Creation and sin

It is rarely possible to meet the demands of a new era with a restatement of the views of previous ages. The attempt to restate positions inevitably changes them. The churches are still generally more concerned with the mechanics of how to proclaim their message than with discovering which aspects of it today need to be prominent. Therapy, and especially human potential, suggest that in the last decade of this century the Church has to discover how to proclaim the reality of God and a new realization of the gravity of sin. Ideas which are promulgated by New Age provide two indicators for this agenda.

First, today's heightened awareness of the totality of the created order will require Christians to offer a doctrine of creation which is not confined to dealing with the language and discoveries of contemporary science alone. We shall return to this theme in the next chapter. Second, we have to grasp what sin would mean in the context of wisdom rather than in that of law and grace.

Much New Age material is similar both in content and style to gnostic thought of the second century. Some specifically looks to that source for its inspiration. Today we are generally more sympathetic to such thinking and are less inclined to see it as a battleground between the 'orthodox' and 'heretics'. The dividing lines have become slimmer. Yet in that period the struggle revolved around the same issues as face us now: creation and the nature of the Creator; sin and the nature of human beings; and wisdom and the way in which new life or salvation may be brought to people.

As Irenaeus, for example, confronts gnostic thinkers he develops his arguments on the basis of a doctrine of creation and not a 'Jesus first' simplicity. Today's churches are in their worship emotionally preoccupied with Jesus and intellectually concerned with the person of Christ. Obviously these are central for Christians. But if we are to engage with the new Gnosticism of the late twentieth century, talk of Jesus cannot be a substitute for a profound application of both mind and heart to the doctrine of God. Irenaeus adopts a straightforward approach to the question: all things are created by God through the Word of God, Jesus Christ. He thus locates any thinking about Jesus in the context of creation. Christians today also need to involve themselves in the same struggle, not so much to confound the new Gnostics as to be able to ground their interpretation of life where it necessarily must be in this day – related to creation and nature. We shall return to these questions below. They are mentioned here, however, since they are raised by the issue of human potential as well as by ecological anxieties. It is important to note this connection at a time when there is a tendency to isolate ecological or 'green' issues from psychological questions and to assume that the solution of the former might mean the diminution of human anxieties.

More importantly the link between God and creation clarifies the question of sin. The Word is connected with the theme of God's wisdom, that outgoing power which was not as mystical as the Spirit but which seems to have been the present manifestation of that God who necessarily remains beyond. The danger of an excessive preoccupation with Jesus and the Spirit alone – the mark of many modern churches – is that God becomes too accessible and the mystery becomes too magical. If the concept of God is reduced to that of Jesus, then it is not surprising that many find the Christian proclamation irrelevant to their fears about themselves and the world of which they are part. To this major worry Jesus is unequivocally not the answer, whatever posters and car stickers may proclaim. Similarly, the simplicities of so-called Spirit-filled churches may have instantaneous appeal, but they reduce the mystery of God to the quasi-magical.

When, however, we bring the idea of wisdom to bear on our reflections on the human condition and specifically the belief in sin we can put therapeutically based ideas in a new context. Therapy is generally oriented towards the past: if we can set right what has gone awry, then we shall live better and more competently. Human potential appears more future-directed, although it is scarcely that different, with its theme of our being able to bring about change when we discover hidden powers that we each possess. Yet both are only partially true. Even the most simplistic view of religious conversion acknowledges that converts are not immune from the afflictions of their former lives, however profoundly these have been forgiven. And many will testify that self-knowledge does not necessarily produce more competent living, either with oneself or with others. But running through every approach is a concern with sin – that is failure or error – and the need for healing or forgiveness.

In the context of wisdom, sin is to be unwise. This is not a mild error; it is a profound disjunction from the God who created both my environment and me. Unwisdom also ignores learning, both inherited and acquired. It is, therefore, sinful not just to make errors of judgement but even more so to ignore evidence from the past and present about how to live. So, for example, to be unwise would be not to learn history as much as to fail to learn from mistakes in handling the environment. It is not, therefore, sinful to damage the ozone layer. That is an error. But it is sinful to fail to learn from this error and so to repeat it. Stupidity, ignoring acquired learning and unthinkingness about my neighbour all constitute sin in the context of wisdom. Then what would be forgiveness?

At this point the Christian faith still has much to offer. Forgiveness occurs in a relationship restored. But Christians see every relationship as multi-dimensional, specifically between the self and God, my neighbour and myself. Forgiveness, therefore, cannot be a matter of my forgiving myself, or my being forgiven by my wronged neighbour alone. It needs to occur at each of these levels: the sinful person needs the forgiveness of his neighbour – a theme most powerfully presented to us in the Jewish tradition. We are faced with the question of restitution and reparation, which is integral to forgiveness. I also, however, need to be able to forgive myself. It is no use not allowing forgiveness to affect me because of a predisposition to pride or, as we might call it, narcissistic desire to be hurt. The restored relationships which come about through the complex experience of forgiveness do not assuage guilt but they do remove the burden of it. In some Christian language, the fact that I have sinned and offended remains and works its effect on the rest of my life. That can be destructive, experienced as wrath and therefore damaging to me. However, in the light of divine forgiveness, the wrath which seems destructive can be experienced as mercy and love, and therefore as cleansing and changing. The distinction between proper guilt (responsibility) and morbid guilt is crucial both in therapy and pastoral ministry.

But for both these forgivenesses to come about, we also need to believe that the wider world which is affected by our activities is also not fatally damaged. For this we need the ultimate forgiveness of God, which is not casually added but is integral to the other parts of the process. This is affirmed and discovered through confession and absolution, whether private or public, individual or corporate. It puts, as it were, the seal on the total process.

Conclusion

The contemporary emphasis on therapy, including human potential, is seductive for the churches. The language of wholeness and healing has religious overtones and sounds implicitly Christian. The connection between salvation and health is obvious. Nevertheless, we may discern in some of the Church's concern with therapy a loss of confidence in its gospel and its rich inheritance. The parallels which we have noted lie not so much in the relation between the gospel and therapeutically derived ideas as between the essential questions of human identity and significance and the interpretations of the gospel.

Practically, therefore, the issue is not whether or not the churches' ministers should engage in therapy but whether in so doing they are in some sort of flight from the profundity of their calling. At a time when religion and God have become a problem for many, to join those who seek to have an immediate and perceptible effect in people's lives looks an attractive option. But it is a mistake if, by so acting, we seek to escape from the struggles of belief and to avoid the profound questions which faith continues to raise. In so doing the pastor is not invited to shut his study door and simply think. The richness of the sacramental tradition and the importance of worship are two of the major areas of skill and activity around which the Church constructs its interpretative ministry.

One reason for the attraction of therapy may be that it lets the Church off the hook of the law/grace axis on which it is impaled. Sin as law-breaking no longer convinces, because the idea of divine law and of offence against it is too external for contemporary human beings. It might seem that the idea of offence or transgression – especially as violation of another's boundaries – could be the way to revitalize the notions of sin, law and grace. Such a paradigm is not dead for all. But for many it seems that the affirmation of autonomy renders such a pattern beyond their experience. The most important indicator, therefore, which the churches may derive from modern therapeutic developments and especially human potential is the need to get behind the law/grace pattern and explore wisdom. This would enable us to recover a sense of the way in which unwisdom is the primary fault, which leads in turn to legal and moral offences.

But in the larger sense, sin, were the term to be used, would today probably refer to the failure of the human race to act responsibly and caringly for and with nature. This aspect, together with its corollary, evil, therefore, will be discussed under that heading in Chapter 6.

NOTES

1 Lasch, *Minimal Self*, p. 95.
2 Ferguson, *Aquarian Conspiracy*, p. 30.
3 See for an extended discussion of this dilemma and its consequences, Shapiro and Carr, *Lost in Familiar Places*.
4 Lasch, *Minimal Self*, p. 184.
5 Wesley Carr, *Brief Encounters: Pastoral Ministry through the Occasional Offices* (London, SPCK, 1985), p. xiii.
6 Figures are not unquestionable evidence, but they can be an indicator. In 1987 24 in every 1000 people regularly attended church, with this number rising to 42 communicants (we might therefore guess about 50/55 per 1000 attenders) on Easter Day. Yet in the same year 289 babies per 1000 live births were baptized in the Church of England and in England and Wales the two Churches solemnized 345 in every 1000 marriages. *Church Statistics* (London, Church Information Office, 1989).
7 On this question see further *The Pastor as Theologian*. Also Wesley Carr, 'Irrationality in Religion', in James Krantz, ed., *Irrationality in Social and Organizational Life* (Washington, A. K. Rice Institute, 1987), pp. 76ff.
8 R. Panikkar, *Worship and Secular Man: an essay on the liturgical nature of man, considering secularization as a major phenomenon of our time and worship as an apparent fact of all times; a study towards an integral anthropology* (London, DLT, 1973), p. 59.
9 G. Wainwright, *Doxology: The Praise of God in Worship, Doctrine and Life* (London, Epworth, 1980), p. 342.
10 The question of authorship does not matter for the purposes of this argument. However these discourses were produced, their construction conforms to the basic style of Jesus' teaching in the

Synoptics. See, still, C. H. Dodd, *Historical Tradition in the Fourth Gospel* (Cambridge, CUP, 1963).

11 B. D. Reed, *The Dynamics of Religion* (London, Darton & Longman Todd, 1978), p. 35.

12 On this approach to worship see further Wesley Carr, *The Pastor as Theologian* (London, SPCK, 1990), especially pp. 213ff.

13 Ferguson, *Aquarian Conspiracy*, pp. 89ff.

14 See further Carr, *Pastor as Theologian*, especially ch. 5.

15 *The Long-Legged Fly* (London, SCM, 1987), p. 75.

16 John V. Taylor, *The Go-Between God* (London, SCM, 1972).

17 Lasch, *Minimal Self*, pp. 256f.

6 | The Green World

Green fervour

'Is Green fervour filling the void being left by the demise of popular religion?' This question was posed by Winston Fletcher in a letter to *The Independent* on 28 September 1989. He drew attention to such resemblances as 'visionary beliefs, a distaste for material values, a commitment to the life hereafter (future generations), and a saintly tendency to turn the other cheek (weaponless defence)'. He concluded by drawing a comparison between green behaviour and some assumptions which were believed to be held by religious people. The subeditor neatly headed the letter 'Green Goddess?'.

Mr Fletcher had spotted something. With remarkable haste and a fair degree of unanimity the Christian churches have endorsed the 'green' approach to ecological issues, even if they remain less certain about the politicizing of the movement as a Green Party.

Since the mid-1970s there has been a growing awareness of an impending ecological crisis. The data may be unclear and the scientific arguments unfinished. But a general feeling that disaster is imminent pervades popular thought and belief. Children and young people are being brought up in this shadow in the same way as their parents grew up with the spectre of nuclear war. The churches have not been immune. Small groups within them have promulgated green ideas for some time. At a grander level the World Council of Churches has initiated a programme called 'Justice, Peace and the Integrity of Creation', which in its amalgam of concerns is not dissimilar to that found in the New Age. For concern for the planet is also a uniting point for many who are involved in New Age thinking. 'The shift to an environmental view involves vastly more than a concern for oak trees. Nowhere is the connectedness of all life more evident than in our awakened ecological conscience. Care of the planet joins economic, legal, political, spiritual, aesthetic and medical issues. It extends to our purchases, choice of family size, recreation.'[1]

Widespread sensitivity to these issues is certainly developing, although it is not clear that they yet constitute a substitute religion. Around ecological and environmental issues the churches and the New Agers have most nearly discovered common ground. Not surprisingly, therefore, it is in this area too that some of the fiercest conflicts have arisen. These have focused on the problem of implicit syncretism and to what extent churches may have, in their enthusiasm for ecological concern, inadvertently imported paganism into the heart of Christian faith and practice. Creation Liturgies, for example, have come under scrutiny for their Christian adequacy.[2] The Methodist Church has endorsed the Rainbow Covenant, but it is uncertain whether the Conference was aware of its Hindu associations and whether this was disguised syncretism. Allan Galloway has pinpointed the issue: 'Certainly we need to make more edifying use of the doctrine of creation to enable man to realize his holy communion with all nature within the covenant of God . . . But this is not to be achieved by adding a dash of piquant paganism to our theology.'[3]

The debate on ecology has certain characteristics which make it attractive. One mark, for example, is the way in which it links the most advanced modern scientific studies with the ordinary person's feelings and capacity to understand. This comes out in the language which is employed: the abstractions of physics take everyday form as 'green', 'greenhouse', 'forests', 'hole' or, above all, 'the weather'. The media may compound such simplicities. But the talk remains that of ordinary people.

For example, since we have all seen trees uprooted and

destroyed and since we also know how long it takes for one to grow, we can conceive the destruction of the rain forests and imagine a world without trees. The idea of a hole in the atmosphere appeals to our primitive sense of our place in the universe. It is a simple idea, which now has the cachet of being scientific – i.e. I do not understand it but 'know' on good authority that it is true. Similarly 'the greenhouse effect' is more comprehensible than entropy or the visions of the end of the universe which cosmologists are constructing from their exploration of its origins.

The green issue, therefore, allows people parity with the experts. When to this we add the inevitable sense of ending and beginning which is associated with these years at the end of a century and, even more, a millennium, then the sense of crisis is heightened. Not only might there be prophetic signs in the heavens; there actually are scientific-ally tested signals of what will happen, unless something is done. And, since the response in quasi-religious fervour becomes almost inevitable, we have an almost perfect amalgam: nature around us, primitive anxieties within us about survival, modern scientific endorsement, with its assurance that our anxieties are not merely unsophisticated, the whole calling for the ardour of religion, without our having to be publicly religious.

Theology and science

There is little that is distinctive about the New Age approach to environmental problems. As we might expect, it adopts a synthetic and holistic attitude. From the Christian perspect-ive, however, a number of questions are raised by its emergence. Since the nineteenth century the connection between science and religion has been extensively studied. The debate has most recently been dominated by the new physics and cosmology. Theologians have made serious efforts to contribute. But the churches have been less successful at creating a theological foundation on which to meet the popular sense that ecological concerns are a serious religious matter. Consequently, Christian attitudes towards the environment tend to be similar to those of the New Age and indeed of many others, even though a nature mysticism is not historically a Judaeo-Christian stance.

The central ecological concern of the New Age is integration. It emphasizes oneness between humankind and the created order and unity within that order itself. The idea of an evolutionary hierarchy is central. Human consciousness cannot be separated from the evolutionary consciousness of every creature, including inanimate material. The ideas of Teilhard de Chardin play a part here, as do some taken from quantum theory. There is little dispute on this point among participants in the debate. Unlike scientists in general, they welcome the proliferation of theories: the more there are, the better the potential for integration. Disagreements arise as to the status of such integration and how it is to be achieved. But the use of Ockham's razor is rare and the opportunity for what scientists would regard as 'spurious scientism' are considerable.[4]

The Judaeo-Christian tradition unequivocally ties human beings to the earth. The final word in the creation story in Genesis 3.19, 'Dust thou art and to dust shalt thou return', possesses both an awful finality and a fundamental reality. Humankind does not consist of a collection of social animals, linked with one another. We are physical material, too, and so our survival is inextricably bound up with the fate of the earth.[5] In this Christianity and New Age reflection are at one.

The next step, however, indicates the divergence. Christian faith affirms that the clue to everything is to be found in the Creator's investment in humankind. It does not reside in any innate or intrinsic aspect of human beings. The idea that men and women are created in the image of God can be used to justify an arrogance and sense of dominance. This is a fair criticism of some of the effects of Christian belief. But it does not follow that it is an inevitable outcome. Once the danger is recognized, we can move to the more important point that this position invites as much exploration of God as it does of mankind. This theme provides the necessary external referent, which if it does not fully inhibit our narcissistic tendencies, at least may control them. Yet again, therefore, as with spirituality and therapy, an issue to which the New Age directs attention becomes for the Church not a problem to which it must have a response but an indicator of the central theme of faith and theology, namely the being of God.

This conviction makes us face the ambiguous nature of our anthropocentricity. This is a key problem which has become increasingly acute during this century. The proliferation of the behavioural sciences is one indicator. We long to know more about ourselves and the way we function. The ambiguity, however, is that such discovery terrifies us and, even when grasped, seems not to bring about the change that we had expected. Christianity obviously gives central place to human beings. The drama of the universe takes place around us and we are involved in it.

The same point, however, can be made about the mixture of nature mysticism and humanistic psychology which characterizes the New Age phenomenon and which is one of its most interesting areas of development. 'Something obvious keeps eluding our civilization, something that involves a reciprocal relationship between nature and psyche, and that we are going to have to grasp if we are to survive as a species. But it hasn't come together yet, and as a result, to use the traditional labels, it is still unclear whether we are entering a new Dark Age or a new Renaissance.'[6] Neither New Age thinking nor traditional Christianity will, therefore, suffice to address today's ecological dilemmas. But that does not mean that Christianity is excluded as a resource with which to face these issues.

Humankind and divine wisdom

The distinctive referent of Christian belief is the incarnation. God becomes man, but without ceasing to be God. This last point often eludes contemporary preaching, possibly because with the preoccupation with human beings and their experience, we have lost sight of a dimension to this doctrine which links it with creation and therefore with nature. In the context of God and creation, the doctrine of the incarnation introduces the distinctive dimension of the idea of divine wisdom. The outgoing, creative energy of God – Wisdom – is singularly present in the person of Jesus Christ. In other words, in this human being there resides not just in a vague sense 'God', but that God in a specific form or style of himself. A simplistic approach to the incarnation leads to a series of contemporary malaises. It merely confirms our innate narcissism; it casually divinizes humankind; and it correspondingly humanizes God. The outcome is truly that man is God, and there is then no escape from or way through the ambiguity of our anthropocentricity.

But according to the idea of the incarnation, in Christ a specific aspect of the divine is revealed, which is, as the writer of John's prologue discerned, 'full of grace and truth' (John 1.14). These divine characteristics of mercy coupled with justice may be summed up as wisdom. For wisdom is outgoing, creative and therefore necessarily merciful. It also has to do with order in both social and ecological life; hence it has also to be just. This has been a neglected facet of Christian thinking and teaching. But today's preoccupation with what it is to be human (the question of grace: how relationships are to be created and sustained) and what it is to act with integrity in creation (the question of truth: pursuit of intrinsic rightness) calls for a recovery of this dimension to theological thought.

In his act of creation, God sent forth wisdom and thus suffuses all that he has made with his creative presence. If, therefore, we wish to speak of the creation in anthropomorphic terms – as we tend to when becoming alert to the way human beings and nature interact – we have here the means to do it. What we today feel we need to say can be said. But connection from humankind to the natural order is not direct. It is through the wisdom of God which distinctively creates the world and embodies its human component in the incarnation. It may be thought that this is a long way round a connection which is more simple and direct. But by creating such space in the way that we think about ourselves in relation to our world, we are saved from idealizing nature (and so worshipping it) or ourselves in relation to nature (and so dominating it).

A panentheistic position, which affirms the pervasive presence of the divine, is thus sustainable. The further point, however, is also necessary: this creative act of God is singularly located in Jesus Christ, the incarnate one, who embodies this wisdom, and hence in human beings, who are remarkable for their unwisdom or sin, an important topic to which we shall return. The result is that the primary focus of critical attention is not God and his created order, however important that is. If it were, we could either be absorbed by it or excluded from it. Instead the focus is always God and humankind.

The ecological importance of 'the neighbour'

Humankind can never be confined to 'me'; my neighbour is included in the reference. This emphasis is potentially more creative than a generalized concern for nature. It offers a larger view and identifiable points for action. In addition any tendency to divinize the planet, the stuff of mythology, is avoided.

Our experienced reality as human beings is primarily of the connection between myself and my neighbour. This is a consequence of the way that we are born. Our first experience, whoever we may be, is of being held, whether by mother, midwife or doctor. The environment is before all else personal. Only later does 'the other' extend to the rest of the world. Our first experience is of another person, a neighbour. The importance of the neighbour is becoming more clearly a central part of the ecological issue. Environmental concerns are being recognized as political and diplomatic rather than solely technical problems seeking solutions. They will be addressed and, if possible, resolved less by mystical, and even scientific, attention to the environment than by what has always been the heart of the Christian proclamation – restructured and restored relations between people. But these are possible only when they are given a transcendent referent. This Christians affirm as God. The gospel sometimes only reaffirms the obvious: the responsibility for change is ours.

Such an argument may sound unduly limited and limiting, until we rediscover the significance of relationships. One theme common to New Age thought and Christianity is that of association or linking. New Age attitudes are all marked by a holistic stance, with an emphasis on the way all things interpenetrate. This is matched by the Christian vision, for example, of the joining of heaven and earth and the removal of all barriers. The concept of 'fulness', or the completion of all things, is included. Then, as now, the theme becomes controversial because of its use in gnostic thought.[7]

A long tradition deriving from these texts affirms the human longing for integration. But longing alone is insufficient; a structure to achieve integration is needed. The Christian term for this is *koinonia*. This is usually translated 'fellowship', but the concept implies more than friendship or association. It describes common feeling which issues in common action. Differences can be and are acknowledged without their being allowed to become divisive. St Paul, for instance, makes much of the Eucharist as lived *koinonia*. It involves a common sharing in the Body of Christ, socially responsible behaviour among the participants, differences (for example, male/female, slave/master) not being divisive, and the whole eucharistic community being enlivened to Christian living in the world. Today's theological discussions between the Roman Catholics and the Anglicans (ARCIC) have not surprisingly discovered in *koinonia* a unifying, if sometimes idealized, theme.

Such language is rich, inspiring but, unless we draw some clarifications, too complex to be useful. *Koinonia*, like 'relate', is too general. One helpful elucidation of 'relate' is available in the distinction between 'relationship' and 'relatedness'. This is essential in any reflection on the themes of creation, nature and of humankind in relation to them.

'Relationship' describes actual encounters and contacts between people or between people and things. 'I–thou' and 'I–it', for instance, have been explicated by Martin Buber and since followed by many. It is possible to be in relationship to something inanimate. Indeed, this belief is an important substratum in much contemporary thinking on ecology. Such a relationship, however, is qualitatively different from that with people: it cannot in the same way as a relationship between me and my neighbour be reciprocal. Ecological mysticism compensates for this by postulating some reciprocity. But for most people this is difficult to discern as a relationship which is directly comparable with one between people. Connection or interaction are more usual ways of conceiving the links between people and their environment.

'Relatedness' is a less concrete concept than 'relationship' and consequently more difficult to grasp. Yet in many ways it is more important for our theme. This word describes those connections which occur as a result of our activity (or even just our existence) and their effects on others, even if we are not directly responsible for them. For example, within a family there is a series of relationships, which oscillate between intimacy and distance: wife/husband; mother/child; father/child; mother/sister, etc. Yet no one of these relationships occurs without its having an impact on all the others. For instance, it is obvious that the relationship between wife and husband affects the way in which brother and sister relate to one another, even though they may not be consciously aware of this. Indeed, the sum of relationships within the family as a whole may affect not only the behaviour of its individual members but may also be having a further effect on other families with whom the individual members are in contact. Yet no individuals may be cognizant of this.

And we can extrapolate this way of thinking to larger scale activities. In a large company, the relationships within one department can be seen to affect what happens in other distant groups, with which there is no direct contact. The floor-sweeper and the managing director, for example, almost certainly have no relationship. They are unlikely to meet in any sense that could be called 'I–thou'. But they stand in a profound relatedness to each other. What each believes and thinks about the other affects their activities and behaviour.[8]

This distinction has been used to clarify interactions between people, for example, in consultancy to commerce.[9] It is, however, a mark of the integrative power of this scheme that something which can be useful to business and other institutions also clarifies the way that human beings connect with their environment. If this link is reduced to one of relationship alone, mysticism and narcissism take over. 'Relationship' encourages attention to a basic dualism – myself and the 'other'. If the other is a deified 'Nature', the focus is on how I commune with that. And if the focus is on the nature side of the relationship, mysticism ensues; if on the 'I' end, then narcissism may follow. The complementary theme of 'relatedness', however, allows us to acknowledge these relationships, in spite of their intrinsic dangers, but not to be locked into them.

One familiar example of this can be seen in the claim which tends to be assumed, if not always articulated, that God is a conservationist. There is a sense, which is encouraged by the sort of thinking associated with New Age as much as by the prevailing feeling of guilt for what men and women have done to the natural world, that God must be on the side of the green approach. Yet this is not obvious. In terms, for example, of the continuance of species, prodigality rather than conservation appears to be the norm. Their continuance seems to depend on what from a human conservationist's perspective looks like profligacy. And the Judaeo-Christian understanding of God confirms this view theologically, whether it be his mercy towards the people of Israel in the Old Testament or the outpourings of his grace according to the writers of the New. God seems to pour out himself without limit for the salvation of his people. The uncritical justification, therefore, of green approaches as if they were patently manifestations of God is a classic instance of delusive narcissism.

The distinction between relationship and relatedness is clarifying here. If we think solely in terms of relationship, we shall draw direct parallels between God's relationship with nature and his relationship with us. If he is prodigal in his mercy towards us, then he will be equally so in relation to the rest of his creation. The stage is then set for a polarity: either we can ignore environmental concerns, since we can assume God will care for his creation; or we can assume, through our relationship with God, that he is, as it were, on our side in what we feel, and so we can enlist him, without any evidence, as a conservationist. This seems to have been the level of argument offered by most Christians, and, as a result, it sounds to many as though the Church is merely leaping belatedly on the latest bandwagon. What is more, the idea of responsibility is also polarized: those who think in this way regard themselves as responsible, while others are treated as irresponsible. We then embark on a life of hectoring self-righteousness, which has little obvious contact with the gospel and probably similarly little impact on the problems.

If, however, we introduce the theme of relatedness, more interesting creative possibilities emerge. Relatedness draws our attention away from primary connections to consider their impact elsewhere. In the light of this concept the realities of life – especially political and institutional reality – can be acknowledged and their importance in dealing with green issues affirmed. We can also be confident in limited action, since no one piece of behaviour can be regarded as containing or dealing with the whole issue. We do not, therefore, have to resign ourselves to a sense of impotence in the face of the enormity of a problem. At the same time, the naive simplicity which suggests that if every relationship is important – i.e. if every one person were to adopt a particular course of action, then the whole world would be a different place – is discounted.

Association with others in this task becomes especially important. This, too, is a theological perception. The pressure on the Church – especially the smaller it seems to become and the more it thinks of itself in a pluralistic society as one body among many – is to believe that it holds the key to life for mankind. It is in danger of proclaiming a so-called unifying gospel, which, so it is held, would, if believed, bring all mankind into a sort of coalition. That this would be the Church is often unstated, but seems to be implicit. But triumphalist thinking of this kind has no place either in the Christian scheme or in questions to do with nature and creation.

One of the chief difficulties in dealing with green issues, however, is the way in which failure is so central. Today's increased concern with the environment goes hand in hand with a sense that our predecessors have in some sense failed. In some green liturgies repentance for the sins of the fathers is considered essential, even if the idea is theologically suspect: it 'feels' right. Any contribution that the Christian Church might make in this area could be not through general ideas of divine goodness, natural order and human stewardship – the main themes to be heard. It may be more through the Church's holding on to the vital perspective contained in ideas of sin and evil.

The significance of sin

Sin and evil may be too casually used in dealing with ecological issues, chiefly because they are inclined to be used of the past (which cannot be altered) or of those to whom environmentalists are opposed, but in place of whose contribution to modern life no alternative is being offered. But any easy use of these concepts can never ring true. Evil has become a confusing and difficult concept at the end of this particular century and sin is no longer part of people's everyday vocabulary.

We find in the New Age material presentations of a more widely-held attitude. This is essentially optimistic: it affirms the importance of the search for integration but bases it upon a practical dualism. If, so the argument runs, we can put two parts of the world or human beings together, then all will be well, or, at least, become better. One example is the need to harmonize the activities of the left and right sides of the brain, its imaginative/creative part with its logical/ordering part. Another instance concerns gender: if we can mobilize female and male attributes so that they complement one another, peace and accord will sweep the world. Human potential contributes much to this theory. Or again, if we so attune ourselves to nature that we can feel resonances with it, then united we and it will discover a beautiful and transformative harmony.

Such ideas are not ridiculous, although they are from time to time ridiculed. There are evidences for such interplay between human beings and the natural world and they would seem to be worth exploring for their own sake. The idea of radical separation between people and their environment may be at least in part a denial of the basic split that runs through each of us. It is easier to see this outside ourselves than inside.[10] But all such stances eventually fail because they lack sufficient conceptual models to cope with pressure of complexity.

To identify a problem may seem to be half way to its solution, but in practice it never is. For instance, it can be helpful in the midst of the stress of human relations to be able to identify when projection is occurring. But that is not enough to solve the problems. Even sophisticated concepts of 'taking back' and so reordering relationships do not change me or the world as much as I might expect. Life and this world demand a more profound and effective response to malign behaviour.

Christianity, in facing those parts of life which are found

to be damaging, has employed the concept of sin. This has played a fundamental role in the development not just of religion but of many aspects of Western culture. At times it has appeared to suggest that (by contrast with Judaism, which has not become so preoccupied) Christianity is morbid, working on an exploitative scheme of proclaimed sin, induced guilt, and manipulated release. There is some truth in this, especially when sin is interpreted as the private possession of an individual. But this is a misunderstanding of sin, especially when it is carried forward to the larger context of society through the application of the idea of corporate or institutional sinfulness, which is becoming a commonplace in the ecological debate.

The idea of sin is like that of sickness – useful for describing the state of an individual but not especially helpful when used in such phrases as 'the sick society'. The medical model does not really fit and its use encourages casual nostrums which do not 'heal'. In today's religion, too, especially in the context to which the emergence of the New Age points us, there is a tendency to avoid the notion of sin, except perhaps in ritual terms. Although confession is still included in public worship, it has been progressively removed from the individual, with the decline of private confession, and in the liturgy has been diminished into a few platitudes. These describe mild feelings of having been wrong, but little sense of offence or iniquity.

There seems to be, however, especially in the green context, the need for some such doctrine. There is a sense that things have gone awry, as is interpreted by the idea of original and pervasive sin. There is also a feeling of our own guilt for contributing to the mess into which our environment is declining. Yet, as always, it seems no use to promulgate the old slogans about sin. Even if they are true, they cannot be heard. But since in any case they chiefly reside in the setting of law and grace, they do not seem to impinge immediately enough for most on environmental questions. Any recall, therefore, to the old ways is futile, since the feelings which undergirded them are no longer to be naturally felt. The way forward here as elsewhere seems to lie in perceiving sin in the context of wisdom.

Sin and wisdom

The concerns of both the New Age and the Christian Church with the created order are similar. They diverge, however, around the interpretation of what has gone wrong. As with human potential, the New Age belief asserts that the failure is in human beings to see themselves as divine and integrated with the divinized nature. The Wicca, for example, acts out the belief in human divinity, which draws its strength from and gives new power to the natural order by identifying with it.

Christians are liable to become confused in this area because they lack a usable paradigm for interpreting the obvious failures in humankind's dealing with the earth. Their original story of creation has God pronouncing that everything is good; their experience suggests something quite contrary. And the notion of the fall, which has classically been interposed to interpret this ambiguity, does not work well in a world in which people find it hard enough to take responsibility for themselves without having to consider how they might be caught up in sinful solidarity with past, present and future generations. In fact, it may be that this particular view of humankind could provide a new focus for interpretation when there is a more widespread recognition of the limitations of autonomy. But that stage has not yet been reached.

The Judaeo-Christian tradition differs from New Age thinking in its presupposition about the natural order. The planet and nature are not something that is given and which possessed original perfection. This is assumed, for example, in the Gaia hypothesis. It is also presented in popular culture through nature programmes on television, such as those made by Sir David Attenborough. Nature is as it is and human beings can relate to it in ways of their choosing.

The reality, however, is more complex. Nature is not something fixed and given, which can be observed, explored and even dissected. It is a fluid notion, constructed from a series of interactions. This much is scarcely disputed today. The fundamental question is twofold: What, if anything, is the life-force that energizes these interactions? Where do human beings, those who have through their observations articulated this construction, fit in?

A Christian answer to the first must include, as we have seen, the idea of God, who permeates his world as divine wisdom. This is one way of joining the idea of nature and of creation with the reality of human existence and its experiences. But these lead to the second question, which is not merely one about coherence and matching between humankind and the world. Since there is so obvious a disjunction, as is not least demonstrated by the need for an informed stance on questions of ecology, it must also take account of incoherence.

The Christian interpretation of what has gone wrong is formulated in terms of sin. This has been in the West largely regarded as a human failing. As a result in the optimism of the New Age it has received little attention. Some contemporary Christian teaching, for instance, polarizes the idea of original blessing and original sin. Optimism that the future can be improved, if we realize our potential, replaces penitence for failing.[11] This, however, is, like much of the New Age optimism, too simplistic. It is not difficult to acknowledge that the classical creation/fall scheme, even as reinterpreted as a 'fall upwards', has been limited. But the evidence both of the world and of our selves as we know them is that serious attention has to be paid to the disjunctions.

In this context a different, but not wholly, new approach to the idea of sin is needed. The view that creation is permeated by divine wisdom, invites us to ask what would be the negative side to this. If the creation manifests divine wisdom, and if that wisdom saturates human life (as well as the rest of the natural order), and if human life shows serious indications of discontinuity with its environment and within itself, then that disjunction is unwisdom.

Unwisdom is not a failure to care for the natural world. We may today beat our breasts for past failures and condemn others for their continued rape of the environment; it is less easy to grasp the economic and social imperatives which led to the present construction of nature. Whatever sin is, it is personal. The story of humankind in Genesis, told through the myth of Adam, stresses that sin is a human failure and not an endemic flaw running through nature which is suddenly exposed. Yet at the same time whatever this human failing is, it has a direct impact on the natural order – a point which is emphasized and elaborated by Paul in Romans 8.

But such an interpretation does not rely on texts alone; it also matches human experience. The sense is becoming increasingly powerful that there is a profound connection between human behaviour and natural disorder. The question is whether we seek to realign that behaviour with a notionally pure natural order – the recovery of primitive relationships which have been lost – or whether we see nature as a construct within which the role of human beings is crucial and potentially positive. Roughly speaking, the former is the stance of the New Age; the latter the Christian approach.

The weakness of the latter, however, is that not only have Christian churches not yet sufficiently thought through their ideas on creation in the light of scientific discoveries and recent experiences, not to mention the challenge of such viewpoints as those espoused by the New Age. They have also not sufficiently rethought the concept of sin.

If sin is only personal failure, the Christian paradigm which then follows tends to be that of law (offence) and grace (forgiveness). The twin themes of Paradise lost and Paradise regained remain powerful. This tradition need not be jettisoned. But in the light of the modern emphasis on green issues, which is given strong spiritual dimensions in the New Age material, and the necessity to pay theological attention to nature, it needs to be set into a new context – the framework of wisdom.

Stress on the idea of wisdom may seem to encourage a drift towards mysticism. In some ways it does: for to see the world as permeated with divinity is itself mystical – a view that poets have frequently serenaded. Mysticism, however, is largely impractical and the wisdom tradition emphasizes this. For wisdom is always earthed (an interesting word in this context). The divinely inspired common sense of the wise person is a key dimension of it. So if to be wise is to perceive and align your way of life with God's revelation – a critical activity, not a fundamentalistic simplicity – unwisdom is represented by a failure to learn, either from the past or from experience.

The prophetic resistance to evil

On its own, however, the concept of sin is insufficient. When we consider ecological issues in the light of a theology of wisdom, they emerge as part of the fundamental problem of the human race and not as a modern novelty. The damage that is done to the environment is not hurting an anthropomorphized creation. The offence is against fellow human beings, both present and future. The response, therefore, will consequently lie with human relations (both relationships and relatedness) rather than any divinizing of the natural order. It is, of course, usually harder to face one's fellow human beings than to create a mythology about the world, not least because in them we confront ourselves.

When we make this claim, we need also to invoke another signficant Christian contribution to this debate, namely the question of evil. New Age thinking, as we have noted, tends to be optimistic. This is in accord with twentieth-century investment in the individual which generally regards people as capable of self-adjustment, if only they can be given sufficient enlightenment and support. This stance emerged in direct contrast with an attitude which seemed to stress the negative aspects of the self and prey on a false sense of guilt. A major stream of Christianity and New Age thinking coincide at this point: put the individual right, through conversion or awakening, and the world should improve. This belief is held against the evidence, for the improvement expected is too great. The idea of sin alone, however precisely understood, and its remedy, whatever nostrum may be offered, is insufficient without a concept of evil.

In the context of wisdom, sin is the corruption of the process of learning – that is, something that happens may lead to serious consequences but can be remedied through forgiveness. By contrast, however, using similar categories, evil is corruption of intent. Both are corruptions, but the motivating context changes. There is a step over a boundary of some sort which so radically adjusts the world that the familiar interpretative tools are inadequate. The corruption of sin comes from inner motivation. This may be conscious, but we are today equally aware that it may be unconscious, often taking the form of projection or projective identi-fication.* Evil, however, which remains mysterious, seems to come from outside the individual, or even a collection of individuals, and mobilizes their individual proclivities almost in spite of themselves.

The Holocaust, for example, even amid all the other slaughter of this century, has become a paradigm for this distinction. That collective 'sins' contributed can scarcely be doubted. But what we can only call an inexplicable 'demonic force' coincided with these in a way which has not yet been understood and probably cannot be. From the perspective of observer, perpetrator and victim alike the Holocaust both involves, because it touches basic parts of the individual,

---

* 'Projective identification' is the process by which individuals project into others parts of themselves which they wish to disown and then deal with them there. The saying of Jesus about 'motes and beams' (Matthew 7.3ff.) seems to draw attention to the damage that this process, if not perceived, may cause.

and mystifies because any attempted explanation based on this assumption, becomes banal. The standard defence of 'I was only obeying orders' tragically demonstrates this, for it is not just the defence of the accused; it is also the pathetic justification of the victim. Somehow both were trapped in something greater than they could or did know.

This is a twentieth-century classic example of the corruption of intent.[12] When facing it, I can find in myself enough of my racist assumptions to know that they may damage others. But for the most part they can, if I so allow, be examined and in some way dealt with. Therapy may help or religion may persuade me. When, however, as the ancients might have said, a daemon, such as produced the Holocaust, sweeps through the world, while my racist attitude undoubtedly contributes to its effect – that is all part of the impact of relatedness – it is as if a force outside me and many others mobilizes this attitude in them and me rather than *vice versa*.

The loss of a way to name this malign power leads to the two strands which are found in New Age thinking and some Christian reflection. These call for individual therapy to deal with the problems of the self and suggest naive notions of the management of natural and supernatural powers, which diminish their significance.[13] Both in their different ways 'play' with evil, because they have no genuine context into which to place it. The Christian tradition has been proved weak at this point. It has personalized sin, connecting it with guilt, and segregated evil, usually into a satanic figure who, although sometimes terrifying, is remote. Thus evil becomes difficult to identify, since we are unsure by which reference points to locate it in relation to ourselves.

In the nature of the case evil cannot be explained. Nevertheless, some such concept is needed, not least in times of uncertainty, even a dark age, as maybe our present context is.[14] Today's perceived ecological crisis is a symptom of such darkness and as such should not be isolated from other factors. Evil, as has been suggested, draws things out of people. Not all such consequences are necessary. For

example, it calls forth prophecy, not least in the environmentalist debate. To this a specifically Christian concept of
prophecy can contribute.

On green issues prophecy tends to be strong on
denunciation. The prophet can see all too clearly what is
wrong, where sin is taking over and where evil appears to
triumph. Because of modern global communications,
prophets can also make links between aspects of the world
which hitherto would certainly have been separate. They
seem, therefore, not too unlike the old prophets, both Jewish
and pagan, as many conceive them.

Such prophets are believed to have thundered with
conviction, 'This is the word of the Lord'. In fact this
certainty was (and is) more illusory than we might
sometimes think. When the compiler of Deuteronomy
describes how to distinguish true prophecy from false, he is
notoriously unhelpful (Deut. 18.21–2): the prophet is
genuine if what he said comes to pass; he is false if it does
not. Anyone can be right with hindsight. And when the
topic is the long-term future of the planet, the prophetic
theory is that there will be no opportunity for such hindsight
and, therefore, there is pressure to claim as certain that
which is hypothetical and to extrapolate illogically, although
with emotional power, from unclear data.

In the welter of such output, it is useful and important to
note that in the Christian tradition prophecy is transformed.
Prophets now bring an interpretative word through which
the congregation is stimulated to greater energy. The model
of Jesus Christ is used to harness their personality to their
prophetic role. In fact, his personality is scarcely known.
We only know that he seems rarely to have had much time
for denunciation. His proclamation of the Kingdom is mostly
one of encouragement linked to demand. Castigation was
reserved for those supposedly within the covenant – the
Pharisees and scribes who were perceived as hypocrites.

So the core issue, especially when dealing with the
necessary, potent but dangerous concept of evil, becomes
hypocrisy, not prophetic clarity. And the prophet gives place

to the martyr – a point which is often lost amid contemporary pressures to effectiveness. Martyrdom is the vindication of integrity and thus the ultimate confronting of hypocrisy. Rather than denounce others – the word of the Lord – the martyr contains anger and anguish in himself, ultimately to the extent of death. Jesus is implicitly seen as the first martyr (Rev. 1.5); Stephen becomes the exemplary disciple; and later Polycarp of Smyrna is made the ideal model. Theirs is the paradigm of the religious authority of prophecy in the Christian tradition which conforms only to the way of the cross.

Such a grasp of prophecy cannot solve the ecological problems of the world. But it provides a way by which to sustain the core ideas of sin and evil, in an area in which they seem to have something to offer, without surrendering to the casual and emotional arguments which sometimes mark it.

Conclusion

The problem is of its nature intractable. But in the religious context of the end of the century any faith that is seriously to offer an interpretation of the self and the world needs to elaborate rather than simplify its thinking. New Age, like much popular ecology, is inadequate because of its inherent optimism about human nature, its uncritical endorsement of norms of autonomy, and its confused trivializing of serious wrong by making the individual the key to the solution or manipulation of unknown powers as the way out.

However, Christianity is also weak here. Its powerful interpretative mythology of Satan has declined just when it might have been useful. The Devil has become the prerogative of sectarian religion and even the notion of sin is feared lest false guilt be induced. But, as has been repeatedly emphasized, merely to reassert old images and ideas is of little use. We have to find ways of sustaining the insights without resorting to the tired metaphors.

One point at which the beginnings of a better interpretation may emerge is if we continue to employ the concept of task. In the context of the task of life, sin becomes the consequences of aberrant behaviour. It need no longer be confused with the dynamics which lay behind that behaviour itself and the implicit competition for being the interpretative base between religion and therapy is largely resolved. Evil, by contrast, is perceived where, before these interactive processes of life are addressed, there is a corruption of intent.

These twin themes offer ways of facing the ecological problems without surrendering the insights of the Enlightenment and redivinizing the planet or nature. They, therefore, avoid the danger of such certainty about complex issues that we explain them and so explain away. And that pitfall is above all escaped, as the Church has consistently recognized in its better moments, through worship.

In connection with the natural world we may discern two streams of tradition in worship. On the one hand there is that of the Benedicite, the Song of the Three Children: 'O all ye works of the Lord, bless ye the Lord; praise him and magnify him for ever.' Its use in public worship goes back to the earliest days of the Church. In this long address to all created things, which reach their apogee in men and women, priests and holy people, everything that is is invited to participate in and especially enjoy the worship of its creator. On the other hand we find the Franciscan tradition. In this animals and elements alike are treated as sisters and brothers of human beings: 'Be thou praised, my Lord, of sister water, of brother fire, of mother earth.'

Perhaps the Benedicite is the better of the two for today. It possesses a ruggedness and sense of differentiation within creation and unity of the whole as seen by its Creator. St Francis' sentimentality leads to loss of difference and the search for an illusory intrinsic unity. But either way, in the swirls of anxiety produced by green issues at the end of the millennium, the humility of the worshipper is the most suitable stance on which to base the humanly-oriented political action on ecological issues, which needs no nature mysticism to sustain it.

NOTES

1   Ferguson, *Aquarian Conspiracy*, pp. 392–3.
2   One which aroused great interest was the 'Creation Festival Liturgy' held at Coventry on 9 October 1988, with the support of the World Wide Fund for Nature and ICOREC. This preceded a Festival of Faith and the Environment at Canterbury in 1989, which also generated anxiety among some Christians.
3   Allan D. Galloway, 'Creation and Covenant', in Richard W. McKinney, ed., *Creation, Christ and Culture* (Edinburgh, T. & T. Clarke, 1976), p. 117, commenting on John Macquarrie's organic model of God's relation to creation in 'Creation and Environment', *Thinking about God*, pp. 142ff.
4   For a systematic account of the interrelation between contemporary scientific theory, religion and metaphysics, including trenchant criticisms of religious naivety, see Ian G. Barbour, *Religion in an Age of Science* (London, SCM, 1990).
5   See Janet Martin Soskice, 'Creation and Relation', *Theology* (1991), pp. 31ff.
6   Morris Berman, *Coming to Our Senses* (London, Bantam, 1989), p. 344.
7   The word used is *pleroma*, which became a technical term in gnostic thought. The debate on the extent to which such thinking is present in the New Testament need not concern us. The majority view now is that it is not.
8   For an extended discussion of the importance of this distinction in many fields see Shapiro and Carr, *Lost in Familiar Places*.
9   For some interesting worked examples see C. L. Cooper, ed., *Organizational Development in the UK and USA* (London, Macmillan, 1977).
10 Michael Balint, *The Basic Fault* (London, Tavistock, 1968).
11 e.g. in the work of Matthew Fox, *Original Blessing* (London, Bear, 1989).
12 There are many books, but one of the most compelling is A. L. Eckhardt and A. R. Eckhardt, *Long Night's Journey into Day. A Revised Retrospective on the Holocaust* (Oxford, Pergamon, 1982); it includes a lengthy bibliography of Jewish and Christian writing on the subject.
13 See Walter Wink, *Naming the Powers* (Philadelphia, Fortress, 1984). He takes issue with my *Angels and Principalities* (Cambridge, CUP, 1974), in ways which I would not accept, but the thrust of his argument underlies what I am here suggesting.
14 See, e.g., Jeffrey Stout, *Ethics after Babel: The Languages of Morals and Their Discontents*. (London, James Clarke, 1990).

7 | Conclusion

Throughout the discussion basic approaches or patterns of activity have been proposed for the Church as it ministers during the decade up to the millennium. There are many signs that we are entering that new era of thought and activity which has been forecast from time to time during the past thirty years. However, even this comment is written with an uncomfortable awareness that this prediction might be as inaccurate as others. We can, however, be reasonably certain that the New Age phenomenon is not likely to set the agenda for modern religious life. But, as we have noted, even if it does not set the agenda, its emergence is a strong indicator of the context in which Christian theology and the Christian Church now will have to exist.

We have discerned three major areas of life in which this comment especially applies: spirituality, therapy (human potential) and the green world. The attitudes to each come together in five indicators of topics to which the Christian Church must give immediate attention as it moves towards the millennium. Each may be briefly outlined.

Simplicity and complexity

The New Age phenomenon is a curious mixture of complexity and simplicity, which seems to form part of its attraction. The complexities, for example, of quantum theory are aligned with the simplicity of vegetarianism or gardening. The Church seems unable to find its gospel in the context of such expectation. The 'simple gospel' beloved of some seems to be simple because it ignores complexities, whether these be of contemporary science, philosophy or biblical criticism.

Simplicity and complexity are mutually exclusive, not inclusive. Yet in order to create such a simple gospel, the complexities (we might say 'richness') of the Christian tradition are ignored. The constant struggle between the accrued traditions of the Church and their immediacy in interpreting contemporary experience is avoided. In so doing, however, not only is the Christian gospel diminished; so also is the notion of experience itself.

The New Age phenomenon directs the Church's attention to the way in which people today seem to need to be able to locate themselves confidently in part of a believed whole. This is a facet of the frame of mind which thinks in terms of networks rather than of institutions. The New Age may be seen as a web of beliefs and ideas, within which any one part is where individuals may locate themselves, aware of the other parts (or at least some of them), but not directly involved with them. Such a way of organizing religious life need not be alien to the Church. For we can conceive this as an institution by which a network is sustained. The danger is that the network is thought of as a collection of people, whereas in the richness of the Christian tradition that network is a range of beliefs and interpretations of them and practices, especially worship and spiritual exercises. The choice facing the Church is whether the richness of the tradition and, we dare say, 'the manifold wisdom of God' (Ephesians 3.10) are to be protected, which leads to a sectarian mentality, or whether they are kept alive by being risked. The continuing problem of baptismal discipline in churches like the Church of England uniquely crystallizes this dilemma and responses to it.

The New Age seems to demand without question risky commitment by the Church to the richness of its inheritance, so that it can, like God himself, be profligate with it.

The divine drama

In each chapter above we have found ourselves directed to worship in some form or other. Sacraments in particular seem to be core elements in the life of the Church for the new age. At the same time, we have noted the dangers of any form of fundamentalism, with its spurious certainties. Nevertheless, it is also clear that our present practices of worship and use of Scripture seem not to be as powerful in their effect as we might expect.

The notion of the world suffused with the active spirit of the divine is a core idea of the New Age and one which has important resonances for Christians. In particular, it reminds the Church of the dynamic nature of both its tradition and its activity. A grasp of this would free the Church's central task of worship from contemporary constraints and help it avoid the limitations of fundamentalism in a conservative era. The connecting theme which should be valuable in this context is 'the divine drama'.

The idea of drama as a way of interpreting Scripture was basic to the Biblical Theology movement. While that ran into the sand for reasons which do not matter here, this idea of the way to approach Scripture needs recovering by all parties in the Church. For conservative use tends to emphasize content at the expense of process, while more liberal stances take the opposite view. This is, however, a case where the instincts of ordinary believers are probably more sound. Their eclecticism is not confined to what they do or do not accept. It is more sophisticated and is a mix of process and content, the two being held together or separated according to the context.

For example, at Christmas people seem willing to let themselves go into the process of the divine drama of the story of the incarnation. The wonder and mystery of this requires suspension of some critical faculties in order to allow other spiritual faculties space to function. So the process of Scripture dominates. At other times, however, the question of content becomes acute and a critical stance towards the process is adopted. Neither is right or wrong: they are held together by the primary notion that in both the divine drama is presented to us.

Drama is, especially in the religious context, never

something that we watch: it is always something into which we are drawn and in which we participate. This has been the criticism of the arts, especially drama, from Plato onwards. It resurfaces at any time of Puritan backlash. Aristotle, for example, saw drama, especially tragedy, as drawing out emotions and purging them, which is one form of involvement. Today's argument about the impact of the media reflect the same concern, but in reverse: the question is to what extent they may give people dangerous models. But both views share concern about imitation.

The involving aspect to drama, however, is important when we consider how the Church may in the next decade handle Scripture and elaborate worship. For it holds together process and content, allowing neither to be elevated to special status, and invites the struggle that follows from such integration to be seen as participation with God and not some failure of belief or commitment. The theme of divine drama roots that diversity which we have mentioned earlier in the activities of the Church.

Attention to the personal

The third dimension to life in this decade and to the life and witness of the Christian Church is attention to the idea of the person. This topic is already beginning to be felt acutely: it will become even more a point of issue. As we have noted, if the Church allows itself to be seduced into a surrender to therapy, it will find itself unable to contribute to people's lives here. For its combination of believed certainty and hence prescription does not fit well with a therapeutic stance. It leads to a sort of informed moralism, which is unsatisfactory for all.

Much contemporary work with people is based on the Delphic motto, 'Know thyself'. Many rewards have come from this twentieth-century emphasis. The danger for the Church, however, is that it can become exclusive both of God and of the neighbour. The contemporary world seems to see the breakout from excessive individualism through stress on relationship with another. But this, as we have regularly noted in the course of this book, is in danger of producing narcissism, which is destructive. The Christian gospel possesses a valuable strength here, provided it does not become enmeshed in therapy. For instead of stressing the pair, it always presents a triad: God and neighbour and self. Relationship between any two of these needs always to include the third as a point of reference.

As an example we may take a contemporary issue which looks like dominating much of the Church's thinking about the person during the coming decade. This is the set of issues raised by consideration of sexuality and gender, on which the Church at the moment has not a strong record. We seem to be recovering in Western society recognition that sexual behaviour and proclivities are not just a private concern. The boundary between public and private behaviour, which for a while had seemed to be clarified by ideas of consent and no hurt, has once again been exposed by the rise in sexually transmitted diseases, among which AIDS is one. Not only are children affected as third parties, but also the welfare of people other than those with the diseases is involved.

This is not the place to examine the problem. But it does appear that for its survival society will need to discover ways of thinking about gender and sexuality which acknowledge that in this area private and public boundaries coincide in uncomfortable ways. Whether the question be marriage as a social and personal institution or the definitions of individual sexuality, the issues will need to be held faithfully by the Church. How to struggle to interim positions without anathemas is a challenge, but one which the Church should be able to take up.

Religion

One issue that arises from the emergence of the New Age is the question of religion. This is already facing the Christian Church through the question of relationships between it and other religions. As we noted, this is no longer a field of theoretical speculation: it is in the pluralist society, especially where lived in our cities, a matter of daily experience, on which attitudes have to be adopted.

Part of the difficulty that the Church faces on this issue may be that it too rapidly moves to dialogue. In part this is because it works from its own institutional presuppositions about the Church and so sees relations with other religions as relations between institutions. These may be represented with or without authority by individuals and sub-groups. But 'dialogue' carries overtones of negotiation and diplomacy. This idea may be too powerful for the present situation, because it allows the participants, at least the Christian Church, to escape from the prior question of the theological significance of religion.

Today's churches seem to be becoming uncomfortable with the messiness of belief and practice, as well as expectation on the part of others, which constitute 'religion'. When this is caught up with ethnic and racial groupings, it becomes even more difficult to address. We might surmise that one fascination of the New Age for some is that it seems to by-pass the problem, by in principle endorsing everything and so allowing the phenomenon of 'religion' to be whatever the believer wishes. This is not, however, how religions work in practice, and were the New Age to become a New Religious Movement (as could happen), this would be a problem.

For the Church, however, the context to which it is pointed is that of religion as a phenomenon and of different belief systems (as eventually institutions) as manifestations of this. The leap to dialogue may be too big for most. For all, however, there is a needful step of what we might call 'experiencing with' – that is, exploration of the nature of the experience that goes under the guise of religion. For the Church, whatever inter-faith relations are formally risked, that might release it from any tendency to an idealized Christianity, which is contrary to its basic gospel, and so make it more open to people of any faith or none.

Political action

The last conclusion concerns the way in which the Church makes a contribution to life in the modern world. This, too, raises questions about the nature of the institution which are profound and complex. The New Age particularly focuses this issue in terms of the environment and our treatment of it – the green issue.

From the above discussion it emerged that the issue was essentially human rather than anything to do with nature. As such, it calls for human – that is ultimately political – action rather than dramatic statements. The size of the universe and the scale of the problem encourage grandiose statements which issue in little or no action. The Church is likely to be caught up in this, too, unless it recovers a sense of itself as holding a richness of faith which makes possible a network of belief. When this becomes clear, then it also becomes obvious that what we have always known about prophetic speech and action remains true. It is not the Church that is prophetic: it is individuals or sub-groups within the Church, sustained by its maintenance of faith, who become prophets. The fact that they tend to denounce the Church is part of the Church's burden of faithfulness. If, however, they are able also to change the world even in small ways, then that burden is necessarily borne.

If, however, the Church exists to enable there to be prophets, it also as an institution stands both under their judgement and in judgement on them. We see instances of this in holding people to reality. For example, no one doubts that it is a worthy aim to save the whales or preserve the Amazonian rain forests. But when such prophecy is uttered in London, it needs to recognize, too, that the quality of life in the inner city is no less important a topic. This is not to compete for importance. But it is a practical reminder that in the Christian tradition prophets, whether extruded by the Church or not, must be in some sense martyrs; that is, their denunciation and clarity has in the end, like that of Christ himself, to be felt in their own bodies as well as in those of others.

Conclusion

These are some of the areas of practical action and reflection to which the Church seems to be pointed by the New Age indicators of its context at the end of this millennium. But they are not issues which, if resolved (however improbably), would alter the Church and its ministry beyond recognition. Such a belief is obviously naive. The genuine future of the Church into the third millennium will lie less in solving insoluble problems than, as always, in sustaining some sense of wonder at the existence of God.

It may be, however, that in the religious, spiritual, personal and political confusions of our era, there is a message from God to his Church. This, as always, comes not from within the Church but from the places where the life of the Church and the context in which it is set jar. In this case, the jarring is with what the New Age represents. The call is to constructive faithfulness to the continuing mercy of God and the generosity of the Christian tradition.

Index